T0273297

Leadership in the Digital Age

BOOK ENDORSEMENTS

We need visionary leadership that leads, and today that is best done digitally. If you're ready to advance now, read this book.

Mark Victor Hansen, co-author of *Chicken Soup for The Soul* /
59 #1 *New York Times* bestsellers
Scottsdale, Arizona, USA

WOW! says it all! This insightful book deals with causes and not the symptoms in the leadership crisis of today. You will be turning page after page wanting more.

Raymond Aaron, *New York Times* top 10 bestselling author
Toronto, Ontario, Canada

This book gives you the "master key" that will unlock a wealth of opportunities and reveal to you the secrets that successful people and top high performers use to create massive growth for themselves and their business. As a result of applying these simple but effective principles provided in this book, you will see a massive jump in your personal and professional performance, more importantly, you will be prepared and ready for the new economic times which lie ahead.

Manny Bains, award-winning author, actor, director,
and success enhancer
Toronto, Ontario, Canada

The digital age is rapidly changing the ways and technology of communication. Centers of influence are therefore changing rapidly. Robert Verbree's book is for any modern leader in the digital world who wants to be a person with integrity, responsible to themselves and others, and who wants to learn what leadership is all about.

Miha Bavec, leadership development expert

Slovenia

A clear and revolutionary insight into leadership in the digital age. This book is a fresh approach that will help you move forward and transcend the mental barriers that keep you from reaching your leadership goals.

Gregor Hocevar, entrepreneur, business owner, motivational speaker, and bestselling author

Slovenia

The title of this book grabbed my attention right away. I love how Robert has taken ideas and lessons from his career in the corporate world and broken down each step of the leadership puzzle for business owners. I highly recommend this book.

Alka Sharma, owner/manager of Alka's Total Fitness, entrepreneur, and coach

Toronto, Ontario, Canada

I strongly recommend reading this book. It is filled with exciting stories, lots of wisdom, and accurate information about leadership skills and how to apply them in everyday life.

Professor Dr. George Grant, PhD, IMD, DHS, MSc, MEd, BSc, CChem, RM

Toronto, Ontario, Canada

Leadership in the Digital Age is a thought-provoking guide full of important information for those of us who want to better our leadership skills now in the early part of the 21st century. An excellent book for all inspiring leaders.

Robert J. Moore, CEO Magnetic Entrepreneur Inc., five-time internationally awarded bestseller, Guinness World Record holder
Toronto, Ontario, Canada

Robert's book is a refreshingly modern approach to an age-old topic, leadership. The book is an excellent accurate guide for anyone who has been called to lead in this new digital world.

Ken Dunn, *Wall Street Journal* bestseller, founder of Authority Factory, www.KenDunn.com
Toronto, Ontario, Canada

Robert Verbree's Leadership in the Digital Age *is a powerful book about how to think and grow in leadership. These ideas can be used at work, at home, in your small business, and in a volunteer capacity. Being the boss and commanding is no longer how success is created; leading by example is. Robert shares valuable insights from his extensive experience. This book provides you with tools that can be implemented immediately in all your relationships, not just in business.*

Dr. Stacey Cooper, founder of Lifestyle Balance Solutions, author of *Heal Your Health Naturally*
Toronto, Ontario, Canada

I love great books, I love great leadership, I love great people, and here I get all these loves. Robert Verbree has earned his stripes in leadership on the front lines of one of the world's toughest jobs, law enforcement. Dive into this book and take the lead in this digital age!

James MacNeil, The REAL Love Guru
Toronto, Ontario, Canada

This book is full of practical, inspiring leadership ideas, the kind you'd hope to hear from a respected mentor over a cup of coffee. May we always be directing others to our true leader!

Grant Del Begio, MD, entrepreneur, and family counselor
Kamloops, British Columbia, Canada

Thank you for sharing your life experiences and powerful insights. These come through loud and clear in this passionate and practical book on leadership. The credibility of the ideas is rock solid, built upon a life and career invested in courageous service and commitment to constant growth and learning.

Anthony Rempel, elementary school principal
Kamloops, British Columbia, Canada

LEADERSHIP
in the
DIGITAL AGE

HOW TO INSPIRE YOUR TEAM

ROBERT J. VERBREE

NEW YORK

LONDON • NASHVILLE • MELBOURNE • VANCOUVER

Leadership in the Digital Age

How to Inspire Your Team

Published in New York, New York, by Morgan James Publishing. Morgan James is a trademark of Morgan James, LLC. www.MorganJamesPublishing.com

Morgan James BOGO™

A **FREE** ebook edition is available for you
or a friend with the purchase of this print book.

CLEARLY SIGN YOUR NAME ABOVE

Instructions to claim your free ebook edition:
1. Visit MorganJamesBOGO.com
2. Sign your name CLEARLY in the space above
3. Complete the form and submit a photo
   of this entire page
4. You or your friend can download the ebook
   to your preferred device

ISBN 9781631953491 paperback
ISBN 9781631953507 eBook
Library of Congress Control Number:
2020947705

Cover Design by:
Christopher Kirk
www.GFSstudio.com

Interior Design by:
Christopher Kirk
www.GFSstudio.com

Scriptures taken from the Holy Bible, New International Version®, NIV®. Copyright © 1973, 1978, 1984, 2011 by Biblica, Inc.™ Used by permission of Zondervan. All rights reserved worldwide. www.zondervan.com. The "NIV" and "New International Version" are trademarks registered in the United States Patent and Trademark Office by Biblica, Inc.™

Morgan James is a proud partner of Habitat for Humanity Peninsula and Greater Williamsburg. Partners in building since 2006.

Get involved today! Visit
MorganJamesPublishing.com/giving-back

CONTENTS

FOREWORD

This is just the right book, written by just the right person, for exactly the right time, namely the times we are going through right now.

That's a pretty big claim, right?

As Einstein said, "Extraordinary claims require extraordinary evidence," and I think I can provide you with some excellent evidence for why Robert Verbree's book is the right book for anyone wanting to improve their leadership skills in today's world.

Let's talk about why his "I've lived it" experience as a cop counts for so much. I can explain it by sharing with you an analogy I experienced as a member of the National Speakers' Association.

I know of two professional speakers who used to give quite similar talks on leadership. The two speakers were equally gifted at speaking. They used all the best speakers' tips, great stories, perfect dramatic delivery, outstanding clarity, and organization. At the end of their talks, if you had been listening to either of them, you would have walked away with great information.

Yet one of them was able to get plenty of gigs at $25,000 a speech.

The other, in contrast, rarely got more than $2,500 a speech.

What was the difference between the two?

Simple. One of them had an "I've lived it" experience. The other was only telling about what he had either studied or heard.

The "I've lived it" guy had lived and breathed what he was talking about. It was from the heart. It came from a deep place. It was delivered with conviction because he really, really, really knew what he was talking about. And because it came from a deeper place in him, it reached a deeper place in the hearts and minds of his audience. People were more ready to listen to him and to believe him. They were more ready to act on what he said.

The audience for the "I've lived it" guy didn't react with just a "hmmm, that's interesting." Rather, their reactions were, "Wow! Yes! That's authentic! It rings true! I trust his advice, and I want to make it part of my life. I'm moved!"

Robert Verbree is like the "I've lived it" guy. Verbree didn't get his deep knowledge just from textbooks and self-help books, although he's read plenty of these. No, he's put in 35 years of work in law enforcement, as well as an abundance of experience in private enterprise. He's experienced what works and what doesn't work. He has a deep, personal experience with all aspects of what he writes about. He's up to the minute on what leadership approaches work today, in the real world.

And that means the advice he shares falls in the category of the speaker who gets $25,000 a talk. Verbree's superpower is that his advice isn't just wise and useful; it's authentic.

I benefited greatly from this book. I bet you will too.

Mitzi Perdue
Salisbury, Maryland

Mitzi Perdue is a businesswoman, author, entrepreneur, and master storyteller. She knows about leadership in business and in the family. Her family background from the Sheraton Hotel Chain and being the wife of Frank Perdue give her these keen insights. She holds degrees from Harvard University and George Washington University, is a past president of the 40,000-member American Agri-Women and was one of the US delegates to the United Nations Conference on Women in Nairobi. These are a few of her remarkable achievements

Chapter 1

INTRODUCTION—
AND A GREAT STORY

Yes—you read that right. I am starting this book with a story.

Why? Simple: everyone likes a good story.

You probably came here looking for an introduction, a fore-word, or one of the other openings that so many nonfiction books make use of. But a story is more interesting than any of them, and this story even more so because it's the story of how this book came to be.

"Wait," you may ask. "What gives you the credibility to write a book on leadership?"

With your permission, I will try to answer that—briefly here, and then in more depth later in the book.

My background is in law enforcement, a very stressful environment, as you might imagine. I served for most of my adult life, starting in 1979 and retiring in 2014—35 years completed. During the first 24 years, I managed multiple events, people, and investigations. There is a simple fact that you quickly learn: working in law enforcement, being the cop on the street, is really all about leadership.

In 2004, after 24 years in the trenches, I received a promotion to a position that is the law enforcement equivalent of an assistant manager. It turned out that the position could have been "acting manager" for most of my time there, as my superior was often away for various reasons. Whether I was an assistant or the man in charge, there was no getting past how busy that assignment was—nor how stressful.

Just four years later, my efforts paid off; I was promoted. My reward was to become the manager of an entire region, with multiple employees reporting to me. However, when I took over, I discovered that it wasn't exactly a reward—there were plenty of challenges that required my leadership to push through. Workflow issues, interference from other departments, caustic employees, and little support from upper management… it was a wonder that this operation ever got anything done. There were many times when I found myself flabbergasted by the multiple problems that were constantly coming at me.

Beyond my law enforcement credentials, I have also been involved in several businesses with my family. My wife, Ruth, and I operated a fitness center and a coffee shop, and in my free time, I worked as a consultant for businesses seeking help with their training and management efforts.

I share all this as a starting point for this book because through my years in law enforcement, business, and consulting, I have recognized a key point that needs to be addressed: There is a leadership crisis in the 21st century—the digital age.

Leadership in the digital age applies to many organizations in our society: the family, businesses of all kinds, volunteer groups, government agencies, everywhere.

Leaders must correctly plant the seeds of significance and instill the correct principles and laws for success. This is an idea we find in many of our ancient texts and scripts.

It's very likely that you, just like me, have—or had—very little or no training when you were first placed into a leadership role. When I had my first opportunity to move into such a position, I thought leadership—with a capital L—was telling people what to do, when to do it, and how to do it. The problem was, in my career, being a good investigator and being liked by the senior managers often became the deciding factor in receiving a promotion. Leadership skills weren't exactly part of the evaluation in many cases.

This did not mean success; in fact, far from it. It often meant that teams wound up working for a micromanager or working for some lame duck who excelled at not causing waves and quietly plugging along towards their promotion to the next level.

Today, in the digital age, this kind of management gap has been taken to a totally different level.

In my career, I decided one day that it was time to make some changes. I recognized that the little management training I did have was based on what I would call "command and control; leadership knows all" type of thinking. I was also facing a different leadership environment that was evolving, pushed forward by younger generations, such as the often-discussed millennials: leadership in the digital age.

This new type of leadership was a far more relaxed style, which mostly—in my opinion—brought better results. Truthfully, though, in the beginning it was a struggle for me. I was convinced there had to be better ideas and techniques out there.

So, I went on a mission to find out what makes a great leader. What I found were mountains of ideas, some good, some bad, and for the most part, entirely unusable. In this book, I want to climb those mountains and shout my results down from the heights. I want to tell you what worked for me and show you, through inspiring and important stories from those who have been there, how to plant the correct seeds and reap the harvest of knowledge.

Everyone can be developed into a good leader. You have to train yourself in leadership, though; you simply can't afford to wait to begin the process until you get promoted or get a new job.

In addition, we will look at being a great leader with technology at the center.

Another book on leadership may be the last thing you would expect, simply because many people have taken a shot at writing on this topic. My observations from 35 years in the law enforcement world, my son's experience in the military, my consulting career, leadership in multiple small businesses and elsewhere, have led me to understand that there is a leadership crisis in our society. Leadership is lacking in families, in education, in business—everywhere we look.

As I came to this realization, I asked myself a simple question, *How can I change this?*

The question lit a fire under me. It gave the drive to make some changes and—now—to write about this experience.

I will admit, the techniques I discuss in this book were learned on the fly. Minimal teaching was given to me when I was initially promoted. Did I get it right all the time? Hah! Not on your life. In fact, I faced many struggles and made lots of mistakes.

As someone who was never really the management type, I managed to pull it off, but it took a lot of hard work to get there. I read many self-help books on this topic, attended courses and seminars, and even worked in mentorship programs several times. I found that for me, it all provided excellent information. Still, most of it was far too detailed, produced strictly for pure self-aggrandizement, or printed in a tome so thick and complicated it was not usable on a daily basis. I also observed that so much of the written advice produced on leadership is targeted towards the corporate world and big business. Yes, most of these principles still apply. Still, my thinking ran this way: Many of us manage or lead smaller groups, own small businesses, or want to be great parents, and while it's nice to read about how a Fortune 500 leader has succeeded in business, something on our level might be a more useful source.

Looking back over this time, I recognize some things that worked for me—and some of the things that didn't work. One of the most important things, in my opinion, is your mindset. Some of the other things I've recognized are tasks like planning your day, trusting your people, creating a team of independent thinkers, and the skill of delegation. That last one is a big one, believe me—we all think that we can do it all ourselves, right? Wrong!

In my practice today, even after leaving my policing career, I continue to use these techniques—in our family business, in my consulting work, and in my volunteer management efforts. They stand strong even now.

Why Is This Book Different?

Are leaders born, or are they made? When you ask people their definition of leadership, most responses tend to be something along the lines of, "It's the boss, or the company owner, telling the employees what to do." Technically correct, but not the most excellent definition, right?

It is hard to get a good definition of what leadership is. Here is one that I tend to think isn't too bad: A leader is the one in charge—

the person who convinces or influences other people to follow. A great leader inspires confidence in other people and moves them to action. How about an excellent one-word definition? Try "influence."

Some people are more gifted than others in areas like leadership skills, but the truth is that anyone who seeks out training and is willing to self-educate can become an influential and effective leader. It isn't just education, information, and details that you need to succeed, though. It is a real-life experience, easily implementable tips to help you through those tough times, and excellent life philosophy.

While I certainly don't have all of the answers that you may be seeking, I feel that my journey, the studies that I've undertaken, and the work that I've put in through my life may help you along in your journey. To that end, I wanted to create a self-help book that is usable every day, with tips that are accessible and easy to use. Hopefully, what you read in the coming pages fits this bill.

Wisdom says you can't be a leader if you take part in the blame game—that habit we have to turn a bad result onto someone else. The problem is, we live in a society of blame and unforgiveness. To make strides forward, the way we've done things up to this point has to end—to open room for better things or better processes to begin.

So, let's get started, shall we? Let's do what successful people do:

Step over and ignore the crap.

Move past blame and the inability to forgive.

Keep moving forward to create a team of independent thinkers who are willing to act.

(I'll explain that trick in the coming chapters.)

A 2020 survey produced by the American Institute of Stress found that today 40 percent of workers reported their job was very or extremely stressful. Twenty-five percent view their jobs as the number one stressor in their lives. Seventy-five percent of employees believe that workers have more on-the-job stress than a generation ago. Twenty-nine percent of workers felt quite a bit or extremely stressed at work.

A surprising 78 percent of workers rate their job stress at a seven or higher on a 10-point scale. Over 50 percent of jobs in North America—in fact, jobs in the entire world—are very stressful. Most people don't leave their job because of low pay—that actually ranks around 5 or 6 on the list. The top reasons people leave their employment, or express dissatisfaction in their jobs, are:

- Not being treated with respect and dignity.
- Being prevented from contributing to the organizations moving forward.
- Not being listened to.
- Not being rewarded with more responsibility.

These are significant stressors in our careers, families, and relationships, which are often impossible to avoid. Many people will stay in their jobs or, similarly, in bad relationships—without tools and support that could assist them because they are afraid of losing their income or their position or maybe even their marriage. Those concerns make sense, but we need to look beyond them and move towards improving outcomes for all people.

This book is about how to think and grow in leadership. It is about how to move from a stressful situation at work, in a volunteer job, or even in your home, and work towards you and the people around you being happy and productive—in small and manageable steps. It is about investing in people, establishing relationships, listening well, and much, much more. These ideas can be used at work, in the home, in your small business, in a volunteer capacity—really, this information can be used in any work situation.

This book is not just intended for leaders or managers; it's designed for everyone and anyone who needs useful tools to manage in high-stress environments, where good leadership is essential. You will be able to tell the boss you've got it under control, your employees will be easier to manage, there will be less stress at home, and throughout your life, you will find a spirit of cooperation.

Sounds good, doesn't it?

What's Ahead?

This book has some unique stories. There are some personal stories from my career over 35 years in the law enforcement world and some great stories from other people I know and have worked with who have put time and effort into becoming better leaders too.

I hope that within these pages, the information you need can be found easily. My goal is to give you the tools to manage in these stressful spaces, whether at work or in the home. These tips have been tested over years and years, in policing, in my businesses, on mission trips, and elsewhere. Many great leaders have used them. Some of these techniques will require you to pursue them further if you want to continue your personal growth; there is just no way to put it all into one book.

I believe that if you aren't growing, then you're dying. My best advice is this: continue growing. This book will give you the start you need.

As we work through the chapters ahead, I hope to keep your attention by presenting various scenarios and working through them. I will summarize things at the end of each chapter, providing you with a useful tool outlining what was covered in straightforward, usable terms.

Don't worry—you won't find anything in this book like workflow management or any of those other boring tools that you might find elsewhere. Blah, blah, blah—that's boring. This book will help you with leadership skills, and for my part, I promise that it will be interesting and engaging as we go through it together.

I hope that as you read through this book, your eyes will get wide and you will have a variety of emotions. This will help you with your self-talk and let you feel how to envision what the differences will look like in your situation. Underline things that you want to implement and make notes; the goal is for this book to be your helpmate whenever you need to get some quick advice. I would also encourage you to read more books on leadership and management—watch for a few suggestions later on.

You have a part in this too—a simple one. I want you to commit that you will read right through this book to the end. In fact, let's pause right here, and I'll give you a blank form to fill in to make this commitment.

I (enter your name) _____
will read this book right to the end.

Great! Now that you've made that commitment, I'll make one to you as well. At the end of this book, you will have much better tools on how to manage your employees, and the boss too—yes, you heard that correctly; you can manage the boss, the assistant managers, all of the folks up the food chain—because they will love your skills and abilities at getting the job done. (Better yet, it makes the boss look good!)

If you stick with this book, you will be a success. I feel so strongly about that, if you are not happy, I'll give you the publisher's personal phone number to call and express your dissatisfaction...actually, maybe I'll save that until later, too. I don't want to get fired this early in the book!

The Traffic Light Test

This book will frequently talk about a technique I use: R-Y-G or the traffic light test. This does add up because I was a traffic cop for most of my law enforcement career!

Red—dead—would this pass being published in a major newspaper on the front page? Would I be in a life-threatening collision in the middle of the intersection if I proceed? Red means dead: don't proceed, and think about what you are saying, or doing, or thinking.

Yellow—wait—yellow means caution. For me, most of the time, when the caution flag is up, it's a no-go. Better to stop and refer to Red.

Green—Go—green light: all is good.

You'll find me using this throughout this book.

Getting Started

First things first: I'd like to encourage you to find the time when you can sit and read this book from cover to cover without interruptions or across two or three sessions. Then go back through a second time and underline the things that are important to you. Our target—mine and yours—is to become a better leader, starting today.

Yes, finding the time to do that is difficult, but it's essential to take that time. Read in the bathtub. Turn off the news. Put your phone down and ignore Facebook for a while. Read this when you're having trouble sleeping (not because it will put you to sleep or anything—quite the opposite!). You'll find the time—you need to.

Let's get started. In fact, in chapter 3, that's what we'll be talking about: getting started. Diving in, talking about "decision time," self-talk, and developing a good mindset. These are key to getting started. And the further in advance that you prepare, the more time you'll have to remedy any unforeseen obstacles that may be brewing.

A Boss or a Leader

by Robert J. Verbree

So, you want to be the boss
My inner voice did say.
And then I learned that real leadership is really the only way.
A Boss, says I, with a smile and prideful glee.
While leaders get the vision and say: the team is we.
A Boss points fingers and barks out commands,
While leaders ask questions and lend a helping hand.
A Boss says go,
A Leader says, let's go.
Leaders love great ideas and give the affirmations that you need,
The Boss says, "No, it sucks," and brings you to your knees.
A Boss abuses people and manipulates each task,
A Leader has mastered the art of inspiration and knows just how to ask.
Have you ever worked for a Boss who screams and acts like a
    wounded bear?
It's hard to understand it all, it really isn't fair.
A Boss thinks culture is something found in yogurt,
They seem to think that everyone is just another no good.
A Leader treats the janitor like the master of his craft,
They know each person by their name and engage as they go past.
So, what would you prefer, world boss or world leader,
religious boss or religious leader.
Seems pretty clear to me,
A Boss is clearly meager

Henry Ford said business committed to service would only have one
problem,

Profits will be embarrassingly large; you'll need some financial guys
to solve them.

So, leadership is a higher call to contribute, work, and dream,

We're here to be fantastic, not just for a paycheck, so it seems.

It's not just about transactions; entrepreneurs see transformation as the
key,

A big R.O.I. and vision so Return on intention we will see.

It is possible to change our ways,

And learn to lead and serve.

And be an inspiration to the world,

big improvement to observe

Chapter 2

ONE WOMAN AND TWO MEN— INSPIRE YOUR PEOPLE, DON'T REQUIRE THEIR OBEDIENCE

Mary Mitzi Perdue

When you first meet Mary Mitzi Perdue, you can tell right away she is sincere, interesting, and fun.

Mitzi is the daughter of a business titan; her father was Ernest Henderson, founder of the Sheraton Hotel chain. She is the widow of another titan; her late husband was poultry magnate Frank Perdue. Notably, and perhaps not a surprise at all, she is also a successful businesswoman in her own right.

From the moment you meet her, it's easy to understand that Mitzi has vast experience dealing with people, a well-developed mindset and firm life philosophy—one of service to the community. I spent several hours with her to try and understand her views on leadership. She has gleaned many ideas and valuable skills over her lifetime; many of her core beliefs started in her family home years ago, as taught by her parents.

Mitzi describes her childhood as one that was blessed beyond imagination, with two parents who loved, respected, and supported each other. These values followed through to their children. This forms one of her core beliefs: Mitzi feels that the best parents can do for society is to be impactful and loving in their children's lives. In the absence of this kind of structure, kids are vulnerable. An unhappy childhood is tough to change.

Good leaders should do everything possible to have and promote stable, impactful families. "My parents put extraordinary effort into guiding the morals of their kids, as well as their outlook on life. Mother was forever reading the Bible to us—that was always our bedtime stories. The Ten Commandments were essential to my mother," Mitzi recalls. "Father always had family hour after church on Sunday, often family band, or simply sharing stories of his parents, his grandparents, ancestors, and the family values."

One story Mitzi especially remembers was a tale about her father's grandfather in the 1800s. He went bankrupt three different times, but he was so honorable that he paid back all his creditors every time before collecting any more wealth himself. He ended up a very wealthy man; he is an excellent example of integrity in business.

"When you are told those stories from childhood, they sink in," Mitzi says. "My parents put enormous effort into teaching us excellent morals, ethics, and spirituality."

Mitzi's father was also the one who helped instill knowledge of business in his daughter. He taught her the difference between stocks and bonds, the importance of knowing that income can be spent, but not the principal, and how terrible it is to live far beyond one's means—and how glorious it is to live frugally.

"I told my husband, Frank, about my father's deliberate, conscious effort to teach us things that would help us get along in life. Frank was also a man who put enormous effort into teaching his kids values... his was a different method, because his personality was different from my father's."

After their marriage, Frank suggested to Mitzi that she write a newsletter which he could give to the children, promoting the values that he wished them to know and those valuable stories learned while growing up. In the end, those newsletters turned out to be very similar to Mitzi's family hour.

"I would interview Frank on things like why honesty is important, his view on prenuptial agreements, what his views were on living below your means, why it is important to be a productive member of society, and how important is it to give back," she says. "He would give wonderful quotable answers to these questions, and I would write them up. The feedback I would get from the children and grandchildren would be that everyone would drop what they were doing and devour the newsletter when the newsletter arrived—what a neat way of transmitting values."

Today, Mitzi has continued that tradition as an important part of her life.

"The more that you know about each other, the more you appreciate each other," she says. "I don't want to paint Frank's family life or my father's family life as perfect, but it was pretty darn good. Mother was very big on 'to whom much is given, much is expected.' This is how she phrased it to us: 'You are here to put back in the bucket.' It's evident to me what 'put back in the bucket' means, but is that clear to everybody?"

"By 'put back in the bucket,' she meant that we had been given so much that it's our job to fill up that bucket again," Mitzi continues. "The bucket of things that flowed to us, it's our job to fill it back up again, with the good things we do for others. Mother said the givers of the world are happy; the takers of the world are miserable."

Frank, in his ethical will, used a phrase that Mitzi often refers to. "If you want to be happy, think about what you can do for somebody else. If you really want to be miserable, think what is owed to you."

When Mitzi thinks about her own life, what is owed to her, she feels that "I am probably not in a state of happiness. When I think of what I can do for others or society, then I am in a much better place. In some ways, I feel the purpose of life is to serve one another."

"Mother always used to say God meant us to be happy, but you have to do the right things like be generous and kind, serve one another, and be in touch with your spiritual side. One of my most core beliefs is that we are here to serve one another."

In the early 1970s, Mitzi was out running and had a runner's high. As she was passing some buttercups in a field, she recalls, "I heard this voice in my head. This voice asked me if I wanted to know the nature of good and evil. I said, yes, I would. It came to me. Good is that which is nourished and energized by the healing, growth, and enlightenment of others. Evil is that which is energized by the pain and stunting the growth of others. A shorter way to say this is: you are energized by good things or bad things."

Later, on another run, Mitzi had another runner's high experience. This time, she says, "The voice asked if I wanted to know the purpose of life. I said yes, I did. The answer I got was: the purpose of life is to give and receive love."

The same thing happened once again, and that third time was again a query about the meaning of life. That third time, Mitzi remembers, "The answer was to serve one another. One of my biggest nuggets from the Bible is: judge a tree by its fruits. Where are you going to get more truth than that?"

According to Mitzi, her father's leadership style was that of the coach. He would share information and knowledge with his family during family hours but would never hammer it home with threats or demands.

"When Father was growing the company from no employees to 20,000, his motto was 'Inspire, don't require.' Whenever Father took over a hotel, I would ask him how he could make hotels a great success during the Great Depression, when everyone else was running away from them. He said, 'It is the people at every level at the Sheraton Hotel chain that makes the hotel a success.' "

Whenever the Sheraton chain would take over a hotel, Ernest Henderson would, Mitzi remembers, ask the staff to gather in the ballroom, and immediately let them know that he wanted them to all keep their jobs. Those people in those hotels knew their jobs better than anyone else—perhaps anyone else in the world. Ernest's job, he would say, was to give them the resources and encouragement they needed and to show the world just how good they were.

Mitzi says her father would tell them, "You will see that in a few months, this will be the most popular, the best-served hotel in the city. Together we will show other people in the city that many other things can turn around too."

That, she says, was a true vision for the employees to see their jobs by.

"They are not just waiting tables, or carrying suitcases, or tending bar, or making beds—no, they are part of a team that is going to show the world that things are going to turn around."

Mitzi's husband, chicken visionary Frank Perdue, had a similar style to Ernest's approach.

"I'm going to call it inspirational leadership, but that sort of equates to coaching, in my mind," she says. "Promptness was one of Frank's characteristics. You could set your watch almost to the second, he was so prompt. Frank would do everything he possibly could to communicate to people how important they were to him. Frank was, at heart, a humble person. He didn't live in a pretentious house, he flew economy class, and he treated everyone with the same sincerity and respect, whether a worker on the line or the president of the United States."

Frank didn't show off, and he didn't need to be flattered. For a man who had so much to boast about, he never did, Mitzi remembers.

"He knew a fantastic number of names. We could go into a processing plant together—and there were 16 processing plants at the time… the number of names that he knew and things that he knew about each employee was just fantastic. I bet he knew thousands and thousands and thousands of names," Mitzi describes. "If we were going through the plant, he would introduce me to someone who was doing some job on the processing line—he would introduce me to Delsy and know Delsy's son just got into college or Tony who in 30 years of work never took a sick day. I used to so admire that when he walked through a plant, and I would often wonder to myself, *How many people with companies his size of 20,000 people would be democratic enough or egalitarian enough to just greet people and ask how they were doing?"*

Frank was observant when he was in his businesses. He would ask employees if they were being treated right and if there was anything they needed. He was the owner of a massive business empire, and every check that his employees cashed had his name on it. But he would never walk around with his nose in the air—his approach was that he and his employees were all team members, doing something important— providing inexpensive poultry for people—and everyone had crucially important roles that Frank respected.

"I believe his employees loved him," Mitzi affirms.

Frank would play another role—and one that Mitzi says she helped encourage, thanks to her background in the hospitality industry—this was an effort to entertain every person who worked for the company in their home.

"After some consideration," she says, "he said 'I like it. Let's do it.' So, a few weeks, later we started about three times a month—pretty much for the next 17 years unless we were travelling—entertaining people a hundred at a time in our home. Frank would often stand behind the buffet table and serve his employees—he would wait on them. Isn't that wonderful?"

"Frank was, I think to the core, egalitarian. I have seen him with several presidents of the United States, and I have seen him with workers on the line—and he treated each with respect."

Ask Mitzi what her most important nugget of wisdom is when it comes to leadership, and she will say that it's important to have a type of leadership that encourages employees to follow not because of authority or command but because you have transferred your vision to them. She refers to it as "pacesetting."

"I felt over and over again that with my attitude and my belief, that I could almost control how the room was responding…I could be timid and doubtful, and that could be one outcome, or I could say, "Hey, this is really gonna work, you will see."

Mitzi also feels that, as part of her motivation and the motivation that she shares with the teams she works with, the Lord has provided her with the desire to increase happiness and decrease misery. That is part of her motivation, and it reminds her of a hymn from her childhood, the words of which are: "Service to man is the road to God; serving the least of them is serving Him."

Self-talk is important—as long as it is positive self-talk, Mitzi advises. "I believe in being upbeat. I am not into undermining myself. I don't do guilt; my view is that anyone trying to guilt you is trying to manipulate you. That makes you a victim, and I don't do victimhood either. I am not here to be manipulated, so don't try to guilt me—it is not going to work."

Power is Mitzi's mindset.

"I have an image of myself when there are obstacles—I am a steamroller, and the obstacle is a mosquito stuck in the tar ahead of me. If I am going to be discouraged by things, I will never go anywhere. Sometimes my steamroller-ness is mitigated by the fact that I do want to be popular. This helps keep things in check."

Trust, Mitzi says, is the absolute most important thing that one needs in a relationship of any kind.

"I am almost clinical about it—'This is a person who doesn't deserve trust,' 'This is a person who is out to stab you in the back.' Test and trust kind of go together here," she advises. "Delegation is almost one of the most important things that you can learn as a leader, as well—because you can't do it all yourself. Anything I can delegate, I will."

Strong relationships are a key to a successful business, Mitzi advises. "Both my late father and my late husband said the entire reason for their success was the people who they worked with. That means they were good at creating engagement and commitment that lead to success. Relationships are all important because when you get it right, you get undreamed-of success."

When dealing with many people, however, it's not surprising that some will be difficult. Conscientiousness is key in working with others, she says.

"The person's words that are not backed up by who they are and what they do are a problem for me. That is a deal-breaker for me. Somebody who is nasty and mean…I consider myself to be a nice person—I really try to be, however, don't cross me," she laughs. "I have a girlfriend who said to me recently that people were always mean to her, but they were never mean to me, and asked why that was. She had a hypothesis: 'They are slightly scared of you,' she said. I think I let off a vibe that I am a really nice gal, and I will work with you, I will support you, but don't cross me."

Mitzi says she goes back to her father's position to be the change in relationships or business: inspire, don't require. "A leader's job is to give people a better vision of themselves. So in the perfect world, I would give people a vision of what they can do and what they can achieve."

Speaking of vision of oneself, another path to success is taking care of the outside of the body as well as the inside.

"I am a passionate believer that the outside is the mirror of the inside, and the inside is a mirror of the outside; it is absolutely worthwhile to be your best—dressing nicely every day does something for your spirits," Mitzi believes.

Along with dress, she encourages that good leaders take the time to exercise. Both her father and husband engaged in physical fitness—and keeping fit takes self-discipline that can be imparted to others. "I like self-discipline," Mitzi says. "At least twice a day and probably more, I am walking up and down the eight flights of stairs in my building."

Declutter your life; she advises—slow down to smell the roses, without having to reach across that heap of junk that has piled up on your desk. Also, declutter your speech, and remove the spicy language that can sometimes emerge.

"I have one big problem with bad language…if I'm thinking, *Oh, my, he just used the F-word,* that means I'm thinking about the profanity he just said, and I'm not listening to the rest of what he is saying. To me, it is very distracting; it takes away from the message. It doesn't add any value."

A crucial part of success is having a sense of honor, Mitzi says. "I'll tell you something I've been trying to do this year—I'm taking a honor course. It is so worthwhile. Frank had an endless sense of honor; I loved being with him because he was always making me laugh."

Finally, Mitzi encourages all leaders never to stop learning because learning is never a bad idea. She practices this advice herself: every single year, she requires herself to complete at least one course of education. That's not a difficult goal for anyone, now, is it?

Mitzi Perdue—Interview Insights

- Coming from a good home where there are two parents is a great strength.
- To whom much is given, much is expected.
- One of my most core beliefs is that we are here to serve one another.
- What a terrible thing it is to live way above your means, and what a glorious thing it is to be frugal and live below your means.
- Inspire your employees to action; don't require it.
- Humility, treating everyone with respect and courtesy, is a huge piece of leadership.
- Project positive energy.
- Obstacles in your journey can also be your biggest success.

Chapter 3

WHAT IS PLAYING IN YOUR HEAD TODAY?

"Before you are a leader, success is all about growing yourself.
When you become a leader, success is all about growing others."
—Jack Welch

"I suppose leadership at one time meant muscles, but today it
means getting along with people."
—Mahatma Gandhi

Outstanding leadership begins with the leader, not the position. Before you can lead others, you must first be able to manage yourself. Simon Sinek says in his book *Leaders Eat Last: Why Some Teams Pull Together and Others Don't*,[1] "How you do anything is how you do everything"—and I agree. The origin of this adage is uncertain. Simon Sinek attributes it to Zen Buddhism. To take this one step further, I would add that indecision or hesitation hurts every single time when it comes time for a decision that needs to be made.

It is better to make a decision, even if it isn't the best decision, because it is always possible to make changes on the way to your destination. Success, or at least 98 percent of it—is getting started.

The importance of making decisions is well documented. Tony Robbins advises that a real decision is measured by the fact that you've taken new action. If no action has been taken, you haven't truly decided.

Andy Andrews is on record as saying, "Successful people make their decisions quickly and change their minds slowly. Failures make their decisions slowly and change their minds quickly." The inimitable Vince Lombardi said, "Winners never quit, and quitters never win."

No matter the decision you make, the result you get is the acid test—every time.

Here is what I want to teach you: it is decision time. Do you want to continue in the chaos that currently surrounds you at your job or at home, or the chaos coming to a place near you—or will you decide it's time for some new ideas?

The real question is: what will you decide, and what can you decide? Your decision can be a life-changing day, a life-changing month, a life-changing year! Most of your day-to-day decisions are basic and low risk but learning to decide and implement those decisions quickly is a great trait to learn.

While most decisions are boring and necessary, some decisions can cause serious stress in your life.

When I finished high school in 1974, I had just turned 17, and my dream was to become a member of the Royal Canadian Mounted Police (RCMP), Canada's national police force. That desire was recorded in my high school yearbook, and you can read it there all these years later: my dream was to join the RCMP, and then, later on, get married.

I've achieved both now, but more on that later.

The RCMP would not even consider an application unless you were at least 18, and it was far more likely to enter the RCMP system in your early twenties. That meant there were two or three years to wait—and many barriers and obstacles that might get in the way in the process. It was a big question and a big decision that loomed ahead of me.

I discussed things with my father, and I decided that I would go to technical school for auto mechanics, which was also a passion of mine. It was a four-year program of school, paired with on-the-job mentoring. It was a challenge, but I pushed hard for those four years and even threw in a welding class in the evening to flesh things out. In the end, I was rewarded with an interprovincial Red Seal certificate that told potential employers across Canada that I was skilled and ready to work.

Truthfully, though, my heart was still bent on becoming an RCMP officer.

I applied when I was 19 years old. It was a long four-year wait before I was accepted, but I did get there, and my firm decision to keep that dream at the top of my mind was what carried me through to being accepted. I went on to serve my country for 35 years, most of which I loved.

It is a fact that your decision is a big piece of what you will achieve. Your brain is a powerful thing—but most people never use the incredible power they have been given. Everyone has this gift but learning how to use this skill starts very early in life.

Whatever you plant in your subconscious mind and then nourish with repetition and emotion will one day become a reality. My story proves this, and I am sure that you may have a similar story that proves this point.

Making a Decision

So, how do you make those tough calls? Let me share a few ideas that I use to help me make these kinds of challenging decisions.

Limit the amount of information you take in—many think that the more information you have, the better position you'll be in to make the best possible decision. I'm not sure that is accurate. It is also factual that you reach a point where you have too much information at some point. Don't overload yourself with too much information; it will be impossible to make a decision.

Reverse your thinking and look at the information from a 180-degree perspective. Think outside yourself for a little while and envision yourself offering advice to your best friend, employee, or a child. Challenge your beliefs. It might sound a bit crazy, but we are so prone to making the same kinds of choices throughout life that challenging yourself and doing the exact opposite is often a great way to get around a problem. Step outside yourself and your comfort zone and use your imagination to test some completely new ideas.

Produce a pro and con list—a pro and con list can sometimes bring clarity. Aren't you sick and tired of being sick and tired with the grind you face every day at work or wherever your stress resides? I certainly know that I was. Time for a pro or con list.

Next, you must become aware that influential leaders always strive to grow and move forward in their lives. Once you make the decision, it's time to put it into action very quickly. Sometimes it's a good decision; sometimes it isn't so good. I've heard it said that if you don't act within four seconds of an idea or thought, the thought will be gone, or fear will drive you back, and you will question your decision and make excuses for why you cannot.

Here is a story from my journal of a decision that wasn't implemented well. Maybe you can relate to this story.

As I walked into the office to assume command of my new unit in July of 2008, I was filled with a flood of different emotions and a racing brain. I knew that my new team was suffering from a lack of leadership without a leader for almost two years before I arrived. My predecessor left that particular unit under a cloud of mystery. The overall challenge for me was that the management at this detachment had a reputation for being very caustic and controlling.

The members of my new command lacked direction. They were all doing their things, and never before had members felt so free to tell their bosses what they thought of them or the situation. It was an interesting time to join the team.

I'm sure that the members of my unit were observing me as we got started—and I'm just as sure that they had very little trust in me, and the process in particular. I was also confident that I would need to learn a new leadership style for the modern era, even at this early point in our relationship.

I was part of the police world shaped like the military has traditionally operated. Here, leadership was defined as telling people what to do. The employees—soldiers, officers—were expected to obey directions immediately. We called our organization a paramilitary organization, but this could be more properly defined as the command-and-control leadership style. I had learned it well over the 29 years I had spent in the RCMP at that point, and the truth was, it was getting less and less effective.

That operation style caused me a lot of grief and problems at times, and I found myself becoming quite weary of it. I wasn't the only one, mind you—even upper management in the organization was looking at the potential benefits of relaxing that command-and-control style, with an eye for moving towards a self-audit system that gave employees the ability to think and act independently.

So, during my first week on that job, I decided to implement a change that was validated by policy. The violation that had occurred to spur this on was a serious infraction of policy, and a change was essential. The problem was how I handled it; I didn't consult my team and instead just boomed out the order like a cannon going off. It was command and control at its finest, and I imagine you can guess how that went…and if you can't, well, here it is: the decision went over like a lead balloon.

Everyone was pissed off.

Why? I didn't use one of the cardinal rules of leadership—effective communication. I'm sure at that point, everyone in the room was thinking, "Oh, here we go, another micromanager." In particular, the millennials were not at all happy—they felt disrespected and like their opinions had been discounted and ignored.

How could I have done this differently? Easy. If I had consulted the team and listened to their input, my decision would have been received and implemented differently. Even at this early point in my command stint, I knew that a different style would be necessary for me to be effective.

I had a decision to make—whether I should change my leadership ideas and style or carry on with what I knew best. Frankly, I could have taken the latter course. I was a senior officer, and I could have said that I didn't want to create any waves as I carried on towards the end of my career—but that just did not sit well with me. I knew it was time to make a decision—and make it different.

Let's take a few minutes here for reflection. I'd like you to take a moment and use your notepaper (you're taking notes, right?) to do the following:

Think about your situation. Where do you need to decide to change?

Take a few minutes to write out what you feel you need to change at this point.

Your Self-Talk

Self-talk is anything you say to yourself, whether in your head or out loud. Your self-talk is a crucial part of your approach to consider. The way you talk to yourself every second of every day is a massive part of how your worldview is shaped.

Self-talk starts to become part of you in your early years, usually learned from parents, close family, and friends. That self-talk can drive you in many different directions. As the inventor and manufacturer Henry Ford said: "Whether you think you can or you think you can't—you're right."

This is true for everyone—and yes, that includes you. Negative self-talk is one of the biggest reasons that people fail at their goals. It can take many forms—a sentence that sounds something like, "I'm not good at this, so I should avoid attempting it for my safety," or "I can never do anything right." It may take on the feel of being a realistic appraisal of a situation—"I just got a C on this promotional test. I guess I'm not good at being a leader."

Our negative self-talk, that inner critic that we all carry with us everywhere we go, may sound a lot like a critical parent or friend from your past. It may be a form of cognitive distortion—those ways in which our mind convinces us that something untrue is, in fact, the truth, causing us to catastrophize, or blame ourselves for small things, or any number of other challenging things.

Negative self-talk happens when that inner dialogue causes us to lose faith in what we're doing—and when we lose faith in ourselves, we lose confidence in our abilities. Without faith in ourselves, we are limited, and there's no way that we can catch that bright star that is our potential. This inner critic diminishes us, and in the process, we lose the ability to create positive change, either in our own lives or those around us.

This is why negative self-talk is a significant source of stress and a limiting factor in success and growth as a leader.

If that's what you want to deal with—that negative voice calling over your shoulder who's telling you that things are too hard, that you aren't up to the task, or whatever—then close this book and carry on as you have up to this point—frankly, there's no way that I can help you move forward right now. But—if you can tell yourself that it's possible to have a good day, and work towards having significant, positive self-talk, then stick around—let's get it done.

How does negative self-talk affect us? Well, there are numerous ways, and they can be quite damaging. One large-scale study found that going over and over a negative thought repeatedly or blaming one-self for adverse events was linked to an increased risk of mental health problems. Focusing on negative thoughts may lead to decreased motivation as well as greater feelings of helplessness. This type of critical inner dialogue has even been linked to depression, so it's something that we need to shake off.

- Frequently engaging in negative self-talk tends to raise stress levels, among many other things. The following are some of the negative consequences of negative self-talk.
- Limited Thinking: You tell yourself you can't do something, and the more you hear it, the more you believe it. What you think about expands.

- Perfectionism: You begin to believe that "great" isn't as good as "perfect" and that perfection is attainable. In contrast, many high achievers tend to do better than their perfectionistic counterparts because they are generally less stressed and are happy with a job well done rather than picking it apart and zeroing in on what could have been better.

- Feelings of Depression: Some research has shown that negative self-talk can lead to a growth of feelings of depression. If left unchecked, this could be quite damaging.

- Relationship Challenges: Whether the constant self-criticism makes you seem needy and insecure or turn your negative self-talk into more general negative habits that bother others, a lack of communication and even a "playful" amount of criticism can take a toll.

So, let's make a change, then. Do a little brainstorming and then write down in a journal what negative self-talk it is that you want to change. Maybe you want to stop arguing with your wife and instead tell her how beautiful she is; perhaps you want to start telling yourself something along the lines of "I am a great leader and teacher." Maybe it's telling yourself that you love yourself—I don't know what it is you want to get across to yourself, but whatever you say can make a profound impact on your day, your week, your month—your life…as well as those of the people you spend your time with.

Writing your thoughts down will prompt more and more inspiration to come to the top of your head from your subconscious mind—this will start your journey in a more positive direction. If you want something to come true, writing it down is an excellent beginning. Something happens when you write it down with your WHY in mind—I find it just amazing.

Six Major Positive Emotions:

- Awe
- Forgiveness
- Joy
- Enthusiasm
- Romance
- Hope

Six Major Negative Emotions:

- Jealousy
- Anger
- Greed
- Fear
- Hatred
- Revenge

Amanda's Story

My friend, Amanda, lives in Vancouver. She works in and manages a sales department. Amanda was struggling with some of her people and herself as well. High stress, a hectic environment, and constant pressure were taking a toll on her and her people.

Upper management always wanted more sales—the next month always had to be better than this month, there was no time for new ideas no matter how good—and on and on and on.

Amanda is a perfectionist; she tends to be very critical of others and their ideas. This goes back to her upbringing in a very strict environment. Employees coming to her always felt her negative energy and low vibration; no one wanted to share new ideas, and relationships on her team were strained. (Vibration, by the way, is one's energetic frequency—low vibration generally means that you have lowered energy and negative emotions, while high vibration often means you're more optimistic, cheerful, and lighting up the room around you!)

Things in her department finally reached a boiling point. Amanda recognized that change was necessary, to her credit, and she understood that the blame game would not work. Moreover, she knew that as a manager, a leader should be someone with a positive influence. After all, as we said previously, leadership can be briefly described as influence—remember?

Where to start was the biggest question.

Amanda recognized and was aware that she needed to make changes first. As she plunged into research on improving her management style, Amanda turned up an article about self-talk that provided suggestions on how to change.

The first step: to decide a change was necessary. Once she had affirmed that yes, she needed to make a shift, Amanda kept track of her self-talk in a journal. It didn't take long for her to notice the problems that were cropping up: her perfectionism, critical spirit, and negative energy. The problems poured out of her notes; she realized it was all carrying over into her work environment.

Amanda was right. Sometimes, it seemed, her negative energy could peel paint off the walls around her. This, she decided, was the spot to make a change.

Note, here, that I did not say "try." Amanda made the conscious decision to change, and she pushed hard to make it work. She became grateful for blessings in her life, for great employees and their ideas, and she complimented them and focused on their gifts. She started a gratitude journal and wrote in it every morning.

Amanda turned herself—and her management style—around in a short time. Just this one little change in her self-talk made a massive difference in how she talked to and treated her employees. It changed her countenance, helped develop great relationships with her team, and she began to love and accept their great ideas.

The whole process was contagious, she found—and she wanted more.

The best part of the results was that relationships were mended, ideas flowed, discontent vaporized, and, soon, her department was on top of the sales ladder at her company.

To me, that is a powerful statement—and worth a shot in your own business or family situation, wouldn't you agree? How you talk to yourself and others is very important to keep in mind. This is a green = go idea!

Changing or Improving Self-Talk

Here's a list of 10 potential questions to ask yourself as you think about your self-talk. You can explore plenty, but these provide an excellent starting point for those who need to work on their self-talk.

- Am I grateful for each day?
- Am I considering: If this was the last day of my life, would I want to do what
- Am I considering: If this was the last day of my life, would I want to do what I am about to do today – would it be that important?
- Am I jumping to conclusions before I know all the facts?
- Am I thinking globally or just thinking of myself?
- Am I blaming myself for something that's not my fault?
- Am I taking something personally that has little or nothing to do with me?

- Am I expecting myself and others to be perfect?
- Am I paying attention to only the negative side of things?
- Am I overestimating the chances of disaster or exaggerating the importance of events?
- Are my thoughts helping or hindering me?

Chapter 4

YOUR MINDSET—
IS IT FIXED OR GROWING?

I'm glad you are still here with me. Thank you for taking the first step and listening to your self-talk. Did you implement some of these ideas, like Amanda did, at work or in your home? It doesn't have to be perfect to start; it is possible to make changes in direction along the way. The main thing is to get started. Don't add time—don't procrastinate. A change of one degree today is a considerable difference in six months and a massive change in 365 days.

Now, let's talk about having a good mindset.

Let's say it's a foggy day outside, and you can only see 100 or so feet ahead. Many would turn back and not take any action—that's one type of mindset. If you think, "I will walk that 100 feet forward, then I will be able to see 100 feet further, and once I'm there, then take the next steps," this is another mindset.

The mindset puzzle is related to your self-talk, but these are two different pieces as well. Remember, self-talk is anything you say to yourself on an ongoing basis, whether in your head or out loud. Mindset is the broader piece, the things that have been programmed into our minds by family, friends, enemies, and circumstances from childhood through to today. The mindsets we adopt have everything to do with our judgment of anything and everything, and it affects our responses.

Did you get that? This is important!

The mindsets we adopt have everything to do with our judgment of anything and everything and how we respond or react to those things in our lives. Whether it is fixed or growing, our mindset is a collection of beliefs and thoughts that make up our mental attitude, inclination, habits, or dispositions. It can predetermine a person's reaction and responses to events, circumstances, and situations. There are a couple of ways that mindsets can develop. If you have a fixed mindset, you do not want to change or see opportunities; but if you have a growth mindset, you want to grow, change, see the possibilities, and become better.

The mindset in leadership can be one of our most significant opportunities. There are times when leadership can be a series of barriers and obstacles, and these obstacles or barriers sometimes can hold the key to your most incredible opportunity. Opportunities are often cleverly disguised as insurmountable problems or barriers. This is where we need to discipline ourselves to see the opportunities that exist everywhere. We need to discipline our mindset.

Let's paint a word picture here to describe just what a good mindset might look like.

Walk to the water cooler in your office—something you do regularly—but walk like there's a rock concert going on in there.

Yeah, I know; what the heck is this guy saying?

Change the description. Know where you are going and how you are going to get there. See the opportunities that are in front of you—like that rock concert at the water cooler—and seize them. Those around you will see what you're doing with those opportunities, and they'll enjoy watching you perform. Your drive will become contagious.

The message here is simple: let everyone see your positive mindset—always!

When I started at my management job, the office atmosphere was very negative—that was the team's mindset. I would ask people around the office how they were doing, and the responses would be along the lines of "I'm here," or a vague "Okay," or a comment about how they couldn't wait until it was 4:00 p.m.—quitting time! That, to me, was entirely the wrong mindset and an unhealthy one.

Why not say, "I am so lucky and blessed to be able to come to work today because I am healthy and able." For me, when I was asked how I was doing on that day, I would always say, "I'm fabulous. If I were any better, I would be triplets." My mindset was that I was good, and even the situation was good.

Slowly my mindset did start to adjust and change the office climate, and in time people were smiling when I came to their workspace. After some time, people said they were fabulous too when asked how they were.

So, how do we define mindset? We could say it is the way that we perceive the world. This affects how we live and the decisions we make every day.

How do we change or significantly improve our mindset?

Reading

So many opportunities are revealed within the pages of quality books, and there is a nearly endless supply of them to take advantage of. Books stimulate your imagination, give you great ideas, and teach you how others have done it successfully—just like this book is doing, I hope!

It has been said that you are not growing if you don't read. I fully agree with that statement. Reading is like the icing on the cake, the socks on feet, the gravy on meat.

Another important thing about reading is that you will open your subconscious mind and, when that happens, you will be amazed at what flows out. You have years of knowledge in there, just waiting to pop out. You have seemingly forgotten more things than you remember—but that's not the case because, with the right stimulation, all that knowledge can be accessed and used to help you grow.

Don't forget to read authors of the past because their insights are still relevant even here in the 21st century. I've always liked the saying, "Don't remove an ancient fence because you are going to find out why it was put there in the first place." Strategies from the past are still valuable and can be thrown into the mixer to bring forth the best knowledge blend. Keep this in mind to guide your shopping habits when looking for that book you need to read.

I choose a variety of books for my reading: those from the past, those that are recommended (there's a pile of titles either written down on a notepad or kept on my phone—I write down recommendations every time, and you should too!), and titles that I just pick up. I decided to read at least one book per week, so that's 52 in a year. You may be saying, "I haven't got time for this!" Well, my mindset—and it could be yours too—is that you don't have time not to.

Reading books expands how you think. I'm glad you have chosen to read this one and add my experiences to your life.

Books, as well, are less of a timewaster than sites like Facebook or other online sources of information—we'll talk about that in a moment.

Media—the Good Part

Living in the Information Age is a real opportunity for anyone who wants to learn more about themselves and the world we live in and improve themselves and the world.

There is just so much out there to learn! I find it addicting. Just seeking out the media can make you an expert in your field if you use it right.

So, how do you pick through it and make the right choices?

Choose good quality videos, audiobooks, online courses, and TED Talks. These should provide you with an excellent start and help you get moving on your journey. Today, it is easy to look up a subject, learn it, and become an expert—just thanks to YouTube! I have done this in several aspects of my exciting life.

Let's say that one day you think to yourself, *I need to learn about X.* You go to YouTube and do a search—and it's incredible the amount of awe-inspiring information that crops up from experts who know the how and why of that particular topic.

Check out online courses. Many of these are available today, both free and paid—but frankly, there are so many free courses and training materials out there that you should be able to learn just about anything if you search for it.

Beyond that, let's look at other sources of material. For example, Audiobooks are a gift; you can listen anywhere and make great use of your time. Listen when walking, in the car, driving to work, or an event. Why waste your time on the news and rock music? Now, there's nothing wrong with the news or your musical choices, but the question that you should ask is, are they making you grow today, or not?

It's that simple. Like anything in your life, this is a choice you need to make: who you will listen to, what information you will gather, and how that information will affect your actions today.

How you do anything is how you do everything. This is another fac-toid you need to keep firmly in mind. To make your vibrational energy rise, look up—way up, as the Friendly Giant used to say. What happens? You smile almost right away—you just can't be a Negative Nelly any longer. I do this often when I start feeling the onset of the "Oh, poor me."

Ensure the media you look at causes your vibration to go up. You will see different and very positive results when you do.

Media—the Bad Part

The fastest-moving media on the planet is found in social media. Most of what we see, hear, and read these days on social media is very harmful and controlling. Even the funny parts that come across often have a crit-ical, cynical, or sarcastic slant.

Don't read this stuff. Do you need to keep track of what's happening somewhere else in the world? Nope—we have enough drama right here where we live if the truth be told.

Instead of surfing social media, spend your time reading a quality book, and learn better ways to do things. Remember that you are the product of the five people you spend your time with—and that counts even in your reading life. Don't let those five people be those on social media who have an ax to grind and are being told what to say. Think for yourself and have an informed thought from the top people in the world through a book, an audiobook, or quality TED Talk, as I suggest above.

The result will be a bigger, brighter you, able to listen to others, and able to respond. It is very easy to go on autopilot, which is fre-quently the path that many people take. Don't you think that's true listening to the news day after day? It feels like it's designed to make you upset, fearful, and unsettled, and to control your thinking. There are even some efforts to tamper with historical facts—offering up opinions instead of facts.

It's essential in those cases to go to the source—look at the trustworthy source, compare it to what's online. Read the histories as they were written, not one written far into the future. They'll help shape your mindset far better than Facebook!

Ten Common Fixed Mindsets You Should Fix Now:

- Either I'm Good at Something or I'm Not.
- I Can't Learn Now; It's Too Late.
- There's No Point in Trying if I'm Going to Fail.
- I Take Feedback as a Personal Attack.
- I Always Struggle With…
- I Feel Threatened/Intimidated by the Success of Others.
- I Can't Make This any Better; It Is What It Is.
- My Current Abilities Are the Measure of My Outcomes.
- I Already Know Everything I Need to Know.
- I've Always Been Told I Can't.

How to Build a Growth Mindset

We know that the best mindset to have is one that grows and that allows for learning and adaptation. A mindset that is fixed becomes stale and difficult to change—definitely not what we want.

Let's look at 12 ways in which you can build a growth mindset.

Be open-minded: A growth mindset requires leaders to be more inclusive of others' unique needs and perspectives.

Be comfortable with ambiguity and uncertainty: Allow risk to be your new best friend. Leaders must embrace uncertainty and see through the ambiguity to find previously unseen opportunities by taking the time to step back and understand why the ambiguity and tension exist.

Be strong in situational awareness: Having situational awareness is the ability to see around, beneath, and beyond what you seek. It's the difference between circular and linear vision. Most leaders don't have a growth mindset because they are out of touch with the situations at hand—their linear vision gets in the way. They act as if they need to be in control rather than activate the people around them to influence more. Circular vision effectively utilizes the organization's resources and assets in ways that guide and drive growth opportunities.

Be prepared and have a greater sense of preparedness: Most leaders are not prepared for transformation. They spend hours planning for it, yet fail to use it in the workplace and marketplace. That's because they fail to anticipate the unexpected.

Be clear on what others expect from your leadership: A growth mindset is ultimately about thinking differently and taking on new, elevated levels of ownership as a leader. As such, people are watching your every move. They are closely paying attention to the decisions you make and why you are making them. They may even be skeptical about them and your ability to solve for the right growth opportunities. Leaders must make sure others understand what they can expect from their leadership. Don't assume they know. Be clear about the path to growth and the role others play to help the organization get there.

Be into ownership: Taking ownership is the difference between being relevant and allowing great ideas to pass you by. A growth mindset demands resiliency and overdelivering value. Don't tolerate complacency. Leaders who tolerate it release the need for them and others to be accountable, which gives the impression that they don't care enough.

Be growing with people: The days of people believing that their leaders have all the answers are gone. In fact, in today's workplace, people feel their leaders are out of touch with reality and perpetuate silos and friction due to their hidden agendas. Today's leaders must grow with their people. They need to eliminate hierarchy and rank and create environments of greater intimacy in which all people can get to know each other so they can grow and evolve together. Leaders must then value the relationships forged and invest in them to keep earning the trust of others.

Be seeking to eliminate mediocrity and complacency: Mediocrity and complacency get in the way of growth. Organizations don't realize that while they encourage their leaders to have a growth mindset, corporate values and workplace cultures have become so outdated that they make it difficult for growth outcomes to take root. Those are environments in which mediocrity and complacency are not only tolerated but thrive!

Be breaking down the walls of disconnection: Disconnected thinking in the workplace is a sure sign that silos are getting in the way of a growth mindset. A growth mindset sees those silos as barriers to growth. Leaders who are hungry for change break down silos and seek alignment to connect the dots of opportunities that currently don't exist.

Be a strong executive presence: Executive presence is about a leader's ability to create a moment or an experience that ignites others to want to know more about them and their plans. Executive presence requires self-trust, confidence, self-awareness, and the ability to navigate the needs of people. It is about earning the right from others over time to explore more meaningful and purposeful business relationships. Simply put, executive presence is not about "you"; it's about others.

Be for inclusion and promote individuality: Inclusion is a system for making sure organizations are welcoming at every level to every individual. Inclusion is about finding like-mindedness in our differences and embracing individuals' unique ideas and ideals. Leaders with a growth mindset have a deep desire to do this and lead with inclusion and embrace individuality as their primary growth strategy.

Be about significance more than just success: Leaders that do not desire to be significant care primarily for recognition. Leaders that desire to be significant care mostly for respect. Recognized leaders appeal to the head where things are quickly forgotten. Respected leaders captivate the heart—and the heart doesn't forget. Leaders with a growth mindset desire to be significant because they want the growth they create to take the organization to places it has never been before. They want change to help their organizations evolve.

Leaders with growth mindsets possess and use all twelve of these traits. Organizations that give people the freedom to do it on their terms for the betterment of the business are the ones that realize the growth transformation promises.

We are transitioning from a knowledge- to a wisdom-based economy; it's no longer just about what you know but what you do with what you know. Allow leaders in your group to do what they know they can do. Let them out of the box.

Hosea's Story

Hosea is the manager of a computer software company based in Rio de Janeiro, Brazil. Naturally, he's a very upbeat person—a real leader who has a healthy growth mindset. However, he started watching the news nightly and became anxious because of what he heard about the economy.

Stocks were up, stocks were down, and there was no end to conflicts. He was having a lot of difficulty coming to terms with losing his own $20,000 in the stock market. To make matters worse, his wife was furious with him for the loss, and the stress carried over from his workday to his family life.

Those who worked with him noticed that he was fearful about making decisions and taking calculated risks now. He was becoming easily angered and seemed almost like a caged rat. His growth mindset had become a fixed mindset. Fear ruled his world and paralyzed his ability to act. Before the downturn in the economy, he loved new ideas and challenges, but at this point everything was about security and safety. At home, he wouldn't let his kids walk to the park or even go to the market for a treat. The stress was even taking a toll upon him physically.

Hosea's best friend, Hugo, wanted to do something. One day he asked, "What is happening to you, Hosea? What are you so fearful and afraid of? Why do you have such a fixed, closed mindset now?" Hosea just shrugged.

Hosea was frustrated. Hosea was stressed out. Eventually, though, he decided on the advice of his best friend—his wife—that maybe it was time for a change, something to help him get off that negative train.

Reading the newspaper and watching the television news daily was not helping Hosea at all—and inwardly, he knew it. He pushed back at changing his routine at first, but the more he considered the possibilities, the more he saw a light glowing in the distance. He stopped listening to the news and started reading books on leadership, and soon his mindset was returning from the fixed approach towards growth once again.

This was a valuable lesson for Hosea, and one he learned quite well. Your mindset can be one of growth, seeing an opportunity, or fixed and negative. The important thing to recognize here is this: it's your choice.

There's a great passage from Joshua 24:15[2] that I often think of: "Choose this day whom you will serve." You can serve by following the masses, or you can change things up and be a contributor.

If there's one thing to take away from this book, it's this: Stop obsessing over the things you cannot influence and begin to make changes to the things you can influence. In most cases, you don't have to go far to do so—because the first thing you can change is yourself.

Chapter 5

YOUR LIFE PHILOSOPHY

So far, we have talked about our decision, our self-talk, and our mindset. I want to continue in this vein by talking about your life philosophy.

You might ask, "Aren't these the same thing, Bob?" Well, yes, in a way—they're closely related, but they also have their differences. Compared to the other things we've discussed so far, the philosophy of life will include your way of defining what is "good" and "bad," what "success" means, what your "purpose" in life is (even if you don't think there is one), whether there is a God, how we should treat each other, and many other things.

Your philosophy of life is a mental framework for understanding how the world works and how you fit into that world around you.

My philosophy has changed over my life, and I will freely admit that it hasn't always been the best or most positive. When I was younger, I would think, "If this is all that job pays, then I am never coming early, staying late, or trying to improve my leadership qualities." That statement gets a Red on the R-Y-G scale, doesn't it? We can, though, call it one approach to a life philosophy. Do you think continuing with this philosophy would have brought good results as I continued down the road of life? Where would I be in a year, two years, or five years if I didn't change my philosophy? Probably right there, in the same place, or potentially stuck in a worse place. It's quite likely in that case I would be a difficult and very stressed-out person. It's likely my health would be affected as well.

Your life philosophy is the major determining factor in how your life works out.

Compared to the one above, another philosophy is this: "I am going to show up early, stay late if possible, and contribute in any way to help myself grow and this company succeed, no matter what the pay is." This one would probably get a Green on the R-Y-G scale. Moving forward with that kind of philosophy and attitude will probably take you further in a year, two years, or five years than our first option.

Edwin C. Barnes—a Driven Philosophy

Let's look into history and explore the philosophy of a young man named Edwin C. Barnes. Napoleon Hill, in his book *Think and Grow Rich*, introduced this story to me, and I think it's a good one to share as an example of succeeding with a strong life philosophy.

Barnes was born in 1877 or so in the American Northwest. He had an ambition, a drive to do something big—work with the great inventor, Thomas Edison. However, Barnes was missing something: inventions, for one, and supplies for another, and rail fare to Orange, New Jersey, was also a limiting factor—he didn't have that either.

In his case, he could have lived by a flawed philosophy; he could have told himself he was useless, that he was poor, that he was not worthy. But instead of giving in to these obstacles, Barnes set a philosophy for himself that was nearly unstoppable.

Most people would have given up at that point. Not Barnes. He went to the train station, was told that he didn't have enough money to continue his journey, but didn't stop—he hopped a freight train and rode it to New Jersey.

Think about it—how driven this man was, the determination he showed even in those circumstances. He had no money, no guarantee he'd ever even meet Edison, and nothing promising to offer if he did. He had absolutely no reason to believe that Edison would work with him in any way.

What he did have, though, was desire—and a good life philosophy.

When he arrived in Orange, Barnes managed to talk his way into a meeting with Edison. The inventor described the meeting as Barnes coming to him looking like "an ordinary tramp, but with an expression and drive that showed true determination to get what he wanted." Edison also opined, according to Hill, that in his experience, "it was when a man was pushing hard, driven by desire even in the face of overwhelming challenges, he was sure to win."

By showing that drive and determination in his philosophy, Barnes won the opportunity he wanted and needed—Edison's interest. Edison saw that Barnes was going places, and he decided to go with him. Not on the first meeting, though—instead, Edison allowed him the opportunity to work in his offices, handling jobs that Edison felt unimportant, but that Barnes relished. The make-work allowed Barnes an opportunity to show off a variety of his intangible assets, all driven by his urge to go into business with Edison—something he held as necessary throughout his life.

Over the months, Barnes continued to develop his mindset and philosophy, but his goal remained unrealized. One day an opportunity arose to help Edison sell his invention, the Ediphone—an early dictation machine—after the regular salesmen showed a dislike for the new tool. Barnes felt that he could sell the machine and took a plan to the inventor himself. Edison gave him that shot he needed.

Barnes took that chance and ran with it. His sales of the Ediphone were so strong that Edison eventually gave him a contract for national distribution and marketing. Hill writes that the association as business partners became so substantial that the slogan "Made by Edison and installed by Barnes" became common.

Edwin C. Barnes took his life philosophy, growth mindset, and many other tools through himself into an uncertain situation and found success in many ways. He discovered the incredible power of thought—and that is a philosophy we all need to consider when working to be a great leader.

Your thoughts and desires must be concrete and congruent with all your drive and determination to succeed to make a difference.[3]

One from My Files

Here is another philosophy that I picked up from my own experiences. Several years ago, I was doing a consulting job for a big company. An overview of their operations showed too many backing-up accidents happening, the cause likely inadequate training and lack of proper procedure. These accidents were entirely avoidable and were costing the company more and more in unnecessary expenses.

It was determined that employees needed to be taught to back up a long-reach trailer, and the passenger in the truck would be required to get out and be a spotter for the driver during the maneuver.

Most of the employees were very grateful for the training provided. Their company was paying them to attend a daylong training session, and if they travelled over a certain distance, the company would pay for their lunch.

One afternoon an older man and his teammate were the next candidates. As soon as I met the older guy, I could tell he had a chip on his shoulder—he didn't want to be there, and frankly, from his attitude, I don't know if he wanted to be anywhere. He was an excellent example of someone who had a poor life philosophy. His time was spent badmouthing the company, belittling other employees, and—worst of all—he knew everything about everything as far as backing up a trailer was concerned (of course)!

Well, I put him through the course, and, no surprise, he failed within the first minute. He wasn't humble about it and began blaming the course's poor design and the lack of more instructors to help. His philosophy was just wrong, and it was affecting his more junior passenger.

Eventually, I had to pull him to the side and tell him if he wasn't interested in being at this training, I could mark him as having failed and that his time would be over. Not only was he a sourpuss to me and everyone else, but he was turning his younger teammate into a sourpuss as well.

It's funny how that works; you put one bad apple into a barrel, and soon the whole barrel is rotten. This is a crucial point to keep in mind: when you have a different philosophy than others, they will belittle and badmouth you. When that happens, you need to stay strong and remember that it is essential to be around people who have the same ideas and a positive attitude.

What Is Your Philosophy?

Your philosophy is a big part of your leadership skills. Who would you want to work for or with: the guy who is always thinking negatively and projecting that the world owes him something; or the open-minded, positive, can-do teachable person?

It's not too hard to answer this question, is it?

Let's do a bit of self-examination here. Are you the negative type who thinks that the world owes you something; or are you the positive and open-minded person? I think I know the answer; most likely, you are optimistic and open-minded. You're here reading this book, after all, and you've decided that it's time to make a change for the better in your life.

Thank you for taking this step to move forward in your life!

How about we take a few minutes to review what we've discussed so far. Your self-talk is that inner voice that provides a running monologue on your life throughout the entire day. This inner voice combines conscious thoughts with unconscious beliefs and biases. It can be an effective or ineffective way for the brain to interpret and process daily experiences. Self-talk is an ongoing conversation connected to your life philosophy, but it is not your life philosophy. Statements like "I love myself" or "I hate myself" would be good examples of self-talk.

Your mindset is the broader piece, the things that have been programmed into your mind by family, friends, enemies, and circumstances from childhood through to today. Your mindset is that collection of thoughts and beliefs that shape your thought habits. And your thought habits affect how you think, what you feel, and what you do. Because they are related to your life philosophy, it also helps you to understand attitude and beliefs. Mindset is how you live your day-to-day life, and somewhat like self-talk, it is a running and ongoing thing. Statements like, "No matter what I do, I'm never right," or, "What can I do better next time to make this work?" are good examples of mindset.

Your life philosophy is the global piece of how you think; said differently, your worldview, your life anchor. Your philosophy drives your mindset and your self-talk. Statements we have heard or learned, like "the economy is bad, the banks charge too much interest, taxes are too high, food is too expensive, if I had more money, I would be happier, this boss doesn't know what he is doing, company policy is terrible, and this job doesn't pay enough" could be examples of this. We have adapted these ideas from what we have heard. These ideas are things we have accepted because we were on autopilot. Your life philosophy will include things like how you decide what is good and bad or what success means and what defines your purpose.

How does this all fit into leadership? Many workers today have negative ideas about their job. I call this the "Thank God It's Friday" mentality, and it is terrible for your growth—as well as deadly for your life philosophy.

Did you know that of the 60,000 to 80,000 thoughts we all have each day, about 80 percent, are negative? Continuing to do what others do without giving it a second thought will not take you where you want to go.

But! What if we changed our thoughts around and had a different philosophy than other people often have? How about being thankful for your job and being willing to stay that extra half-hour at the office without complaining? How about being thankful for your paycheck, thankful for your good work opportunity, thankful you can learn new skills at your job, thankful for your life, thankful for all the opportunities you have, and thankful you can serve and make your boss happy? We can even go a step further. How about being thankful for paying taxes and receiving all the benefits they bring?

See where I'm going with this?

Your life philosophy is the major determining factor in how your life works out. To form a philosophy, you have to use your mind. You have to process all ideas—those many ideas that have come from the life you have lived.

For most of us, collecting those ideas started way back when we were children in school or from our parents and our experiences. Philosophy is like the set of the sail, as entrepreneur and author Jim Rohn would often say. Some people never seem to get their sail up!

"I used to think circumstances ordered my life," Mr. Rohn would say, "but that just isn't true." Did it ever occur to you that your philosophy of life could be bad? That could be a clue as to why you could never set sail.

What do you want out of life? Do you know?

A lot of people have trouble answering this question. We all need a personal philosophy in life, or we risk following the crowd like a bunch of sheep or lemmings, wandering, and responding to random stimuli and information with little or no impact on our long-term goals.

A philosophy of life is an overall vision or attitude toward life and the purpose of it. All human activities are limited by time and death. But somehow, we forget this. We all tend to fill up our time with distractions, and we never ask ourselves if it is important.

Said another way, we repeat the same mistakes over and over. For instance, we may eat too much red meat over a long period of time and not pay attention to the fact that this causes weight gain and high cholesterol, potentially with severe effects next year—or a few years down the road. One mistake today doesn't seem bad, but continued over the years it can mean disaster.

Without a personal life philosophy, we end up living without direction. This is true in all leadership areas, whether at your small business, at home, or working in industry. Doing the same things over and over will not result in positive changes and, it's often been said, is the definition of insanity.

How about this for yet another example of a philosophy?

A man walks into the waiting area of an airport. While he is waiting there for his flight, he is people watching. He notices a man sitting in the waiting area with a scowl on his face, and most notably, his wedding ring is on his middle finger, not on his ring finger. This seemed strange, but he didn't feel inclined to ask him why. Later, wouldn't you know it—when he gets his seat on the plane, the man he had observed is sitting right next to him.

After takeoff, he has to ask, "Why do you have your wedding ring on the wrong finger?" The man quickly replies, "I married the wrong woman."

You can see another philosophy of life here. His scowl says a lot, his attitude says a lot, and his ring on the wrong finger says even more. Would you think that he is happy in his life? Would he be an easy employee to manage, a good father and husband? Probably not. Does he have the power to change this? Absolutely!

An ancient text tells us about how ants work—in fact, you may even call their busy nature their philosophy—the ant philosophy. Ants, through that philosophy, can teach us how to be self-motivated. They have no boss, no captain, overseer, or ruler. They go around all and any obstacles. Ants think about fall and winter all summer. They prepare for what is coming next. No one carries a whip behind an ant to ensure the work gets done. There are no timecards in the anthill, no unions, and no laziness. No ant mothers nag their babies to get out of bed. These creatures are self-motivated and need no captain to ensure they get their work done. Why? Their work is for their good!

Ants teach us to look ahead. In the summer and the harvest, food is plentiful, yet the ant refuses to take it easy. Instead, they work harder, storing up against the coming time of scarcity. They prepare their food in the summer and harvest all fall. Ants teach us the value of hard work and the ability to stick to the task at hand. Ants know somehow that laziness will lead to poverty, with no exceptions. But there are no poor ants; their hard work sustains them!

Robert Byrne once observed, "The purpose of life is a life of purpose." Having a purpose is life changing. To get somewhere, you need to define your end goal. That is essential. And the sooner you define it, the clearer everything else will become. A life without a purpose is a life without a destination. Think of a ship leaving port without a captain and crew, sailing full speed ahead without a course or destination. Ultimately it will crash, or there will be a disaster. Now think of a ship with a crew and a captain, and a charted course. It will get to its destination, even if changes in direction or corrections are necessary. Finding the right direction in life is a massive factor for all of us. What do you look forward to in life? Living without purpose is dangerous.

In his book *Man's Search for Meaning*,[4] Viktor Frankl says, "Those who have a 'why' to live, can bear with almost any 'how.' " Once you have defined your aims and what you want, it is easier to deal with doubts. It's easier not to get distracted from what is essential, keep your focus, and keep moving. Only sustained movement in one direction can bring tangible results.

It's hard to maintain any momentum if your direction lacks definition. To reach big goals, you need time, during which you must continue moving in your chosen direction, not veering off course. Defining your direction as early as possible is the most critical decision in your life. Living "on purpose" means you live intentionally.

Napoleon Hill once said, "There is one quality that one must possess to win, and that is definiteness of purpose, the knowledge of what one wants, and a burning desire to possess it."

To get what you want, you have to choose one direction and move towards it, continually improving over a prolonged period of time. Maximum speed and output require a precise framework; another way, mastery takes time, study, and practice.

People who have made genuine leadership changes and managed to succeed in challenging goals are not stronger, more intelligent, or more fearless than you. The only difference is their decision to act in the direction of their dreams. A strong sense of purpose fuels your motivation.

Successful people have a definite sense of direction. They have a clear understanding of what success means to them. Everything they do is consistent with their goals. They look forward and decide where they want to be. Their day-to-day actions help them move closer to their vision.

Clarity changes everything. Clarity of purpose challenges you to do better and commit to actions that get you closer to the one thing you want in life. With clarity, you can pull together resources, ideas, and people for a common cause. Without it, there is wasted effort and even chaos.

Your direction defines what you do every day. Clarifying not only your purpose but also your direction reinforces your ultimate life purpose. You should have a clear understanding of what you want next month, next quarter, or next year. Think about it. When you feel unclear about a goal, you have difficulty achieving it. And if you don't know why you should do something, you lack the commitment to taking action.

To develop your clarity of purpose, let's take a moment and do these things:

- Define what success means to you personally.
- What does overall success mean to you?

- Create a vivid mental image of you as a success. This image should be as vivid as you can make it.
- Write out your vivid mental image on a notepad. Clarify your values.
- Write out your values too.

Be Clear on What You Want

Getting clear about what you want is a process of trial and error. The only way to be sure of what you want is to get in there and give it a shot. Try it. Then ask yourself afterward, *Do I like this?*

Get a journal and put down your feelings, thoughts, actions, and behaviors. Use what you write as a way to pinpoint areas you are continually exploring. Evaluate your results continually. What steps, ideas, beliefs, and behaviors are you attracted to the most? The key is to do more of what you enjoy and what brings out the very best in you, and you will continually clarify what you want to do, be, and have in life.

People who continually strive to achieve something meaningful in life crave clarity. It's the only way to reach deeper into yourself to find out what makes you come alive.

You may start from somewhere confusing because you probably like to do a lot of things. But once you define your purpose, you will become unstoppable. Successful people have a definite sense of direction. They have a clear understanding of what success means to them.

Everything they do is consistent with their goals. They look forward and decide where they want to be. Their day-to-day actions help them move closer to their vision. Once you find your why, you will be more careful and selective about your daily activities. Indeed, only when you know your "why" will you find the courage to take risks needed to get ahead, stay motivated when the chips are down, and move your life onto an entirely new, more challenging, and more rewarding trajectory.

These Simple Philosophies to Guide Your Life:

- Life is about solving problems, and every obstacle is the way forward.
- You are the author of your own life.
- Make improvements, not excuses.
- Self-care comes first. If you're not healthy, it's tough to be happy.
- Life is short. Do what brings out the best in you.
- Question your assumptions at all times.
- Effort matters more than skill or talent.
- It pays to create your certainty.
- Commitment, resilience, and perseverance will take you far.

The ability to critically think things through is essential. Here are some things I do that keep me grounded and help me understand my purpose and my why.

I have a gratitude journal, which I write in every day. I list no fewer than 15 things I am grateful for each and every day. Typically, people complain and have nothing but negative comments about everything, which can negatively tone the entire day. I am thankful and grateful for all that I have been blessed with.

Another compelling thing to do is take off to the poor side of town on occasion and walk around there. I try to talk to the people there and understand what happened to them and their life philosophy. I always come away humbled and thankful. This is an idea that keeps me centered.

My wife and I recently learned about a need. A friend of ours in another country needed money for food, and his means of earning money, driving a taxi, was on hold because the engine in his car had broken down and was not repairable. I got busy and bought and sold some vehicles to earn extra income, and then sent him that money to purchase a new car. There were many obstacles along the way—maddening, knock-you-off-your-stance obstacles—but we prevailed and, in the end, were able to pull that together and ensure he had a vehicle. Now he can earn money and look after himself and his family once again.

My life philosophy is to help those who have less and who are struggling. This gives me great joy and fulfillment.

Changing the Culture

A recent study by McKinsey and Company points to self-talk, mindset, and philosophy as perhaps the most dangerous enemies of change and the most important aspects of leadership training programs. Some call this "the culture."

The organization where I worked for 35 years has a culture of command and control. Your organization, small business, or home has a culture as well.

It's essential to get a handle on the deep-rooted beliefs in your group, no matter what it is, and understand where they came from—and why they're so crucial to your team. Trying to change these without that proper understanding might just be an uphill battle that will slow you down.

There's no way that new ideas can be generated and no way that you can guide them from a leadership perspective if there is pressure to cling to the existing mindset. Trying to force a new mindset can be just as challenging. As a leader, you need to push the envelope and provide encouragement and influence to each individual in your group—by showing them how to move forward.

If you break away from the old standby approach, how things have always been done, then you will be able to move forward. The challenge will be to bring the rest of the team along with you—to break the chains of that culture, teach them a better approach, and encourage them forward. It all has to come from one place, though: where you are now. What better place to start, right?

As we move onward from here, we will be looking at ways to move forward because it's a universal challenge; every leader needs to confront this at some time in their career.

One way to look at this is to consider culture change as a kind of marketing opportunity. As the leader, you start by working with two people and encouraging their buy-in to become great leaders. Then you send them along to share their newfound knowledge with two more people. They carry that on, and on, and on—and soon you've got quite an army of leaders to work with!

What's Your Story?

Here is an excellent mental picture of decision, self-talk, mindset, and life philosophy: we could think of it like a picture hanging on a wall. Looking at the wall with the picture on it would represent your decision. The picture in the frame is your self-talk, the frame around the picture is your mindset, and the wall where the picture hangs is your life philosophy.

Now, I'd like you to take action. Write your own story—just like the Mitzi Perdue interview in chapter 2.

Here's the list of questions that I used for all of the interviews you'll read here. Take a moment and interview yourself—you will hear what you're saying to yourself moment to moment, daily, and overall.

- When and where were you born?

- Tell me a little about your upbringing and your gifts.
- What field of work were you involved in? Describe it.
- What is your leadership style?
- Tell me about a mentor in your life and the effect that had on your leadership,
- growth, and career.
- What is your best leadership nugget?
- Also, look at how you define these leadership terms:
- Self-talk.
- Mindset.
- Life philosophy.
- Vision, mission, and goals.
- Know and listen, test, trust, and delegate.
- Dealing with difficult people.
- What can you do to be the change?
- Relationships.
- Dress for success.
- Exercise.
- Remove clutter from your life.
- Profanity and bad language.
- Having a sense of honor.

A Day in the City

By Robert J. Verbree

Today out walking, relaxing, and people watching.
I observed!
Some people slouching, some walking and running and sitting,
each with their heads down, oh the life they are missing!
Missing all the abundance that we see around town.
All the smiling faces and flowers and trees with their blossoms.
The brilliance of air and the colors so awesome.
The short and the fat and the tall and the skinny.
In a world made for fellowship with laughter and kidding.
As I gazed, one walked into the traffic without looking
until a horn changed the course in a second.
Another walking his kids just ignoring their words and their actions.
A mother nursing and missing the coos and expressions.
Later in the day, driving on the freeway at 80, I observe a driver watch-
ing a movie,
paying attention to things other than driving.
Is it right to be that stupid? I ask myself.
It's been said great minds discuss big ideas and dreams,
The average talk about the high prices of gasoline and weather and
things.
At the lowest levels, people discuss other people.
So what was it I was seeing this day?
An almost total lack of expression without actions and speech, just an
emoji.
A total lack of engagement and direction.

Conversations sent to a friend at your side, without woo-hooing and
  smile,
Just fast-moving fingers that can't pause for a while.
The viewing of a screen.
One-word answers, ya and okay, abbreviations ttyl, cya, and kk.
I thought this is crazy; there is something I've missed!
Are we becoming like robots, emotionless stiffs?
No, this is a mindset I said to myself,
But changing our self-talk could definitely help!
But wait, I saw hope out the corner of my eye,
Some kids who were screaming and skylarking nearby.
Yes, I thought, the creator of all things will prevail in this mess.
It is said that he works all things for good, so I need not worry or fret.
Wisdom says, live in the present moment.
My thought was okay!
I need not be stressed; he who sees all will continually bless.
Now for a while, I must keep opening the doors,
which sustain me and keep me engaged in this mess.
Yes, there is nothing new under the sun. Is there?
It's all been here before, the same things, just different packaging,
  I guess.

Chapter 6

THE IMPORTANCE OF RELATIONSHIPS

Harry Bicknell

When you meet Harry Bicknell, you feel at ease right away. Harry has built his life around creating relationships—and he is very, very good at it. I'm convinced that telling his story will make one great nugget for you to consider during this journey to better leadership.

Harry Bicknell is a semiretired pastor. If there's any career in which you learn to be a good listener and relationship builder, that is undoubtedly one.

He has served in his current church as the senior pastor for 22 years and then as an associate pastor for three years. Today he works parttime looking after seniors.

Born in Vancouver, British Columbia, in the early 1950s, Harry's family moved further out into the Fraser Valley when he was six, settling in what was then a more rural part of the province, Surrey. (Surrey today is far from rural—for the most part—how things change!)

Harry was a typical teen who loved sports and being outdoors. He says that he's quite thankful for the teachers in his life who helped him get through his schooling—school was not at the top of his priority list in his early years. That changed over time, and today he is an avid reader and learner.

Harry's parents were quiet, unassuming, and hardworking, all qualities that they imparted to their son along the way. It was a different quality that steered him towards his future; however, Harry remembers that he had a spiritual awakening at the age of 18 and began reading the Bible for the first time.

Proverbs was Harry's first reading in the Good Book, and today remains his favorite. He reads a chapter of Proverbs every day and has done so every day for the last 30 years.

While it was apparent that Harry had a strong relationship with God at that age, life carried him off on a different route. His first adult job was in sawmills, where he worked for a little more than a year before heading to Europe to spend a year there. Coming back to North America, Harry spent the next 25 months—straight, with nothing but weekends off—working in construction to make enough for his schooling. Eventually, he found himself hired as the youth pastor at a Surrey church.

The senior pastor there, Calvin Netterfield, took Harry under his wing and acted as a mentor for the younger pastor. Harry, under Calvin's mentorship and guidance, grew into several different roles.

Describing his mentor, Harry says that Calvin was a servant—someone who would never be easily offended and who loved his church.

Calvin never talked about problems—he talked about solutions. Calvin's role was to promote other people around him vigorously. In his career, Calvin focused on making the others around him better rather than glorifying himself. He was recognized for what he did, and he continues to be a great encourager of those around him.

Harry describes Calvin as a longtime reader, and he continues to read plenty today—something that brings with it a broad perspective on the world as a whole. Reading is a valuable source of many benefits, including finding more mentors, Harry notes.

Of the many nuggets of wisdom that Calvin has passed along to Harry, one of the more important ones that Harry points to is this: there is always a way to make things work—there is still a solution to every challenge.

He also learned beneficial skills such as listening well, the warning to beware of one's dark side, and one of the most important—building relationships while giving oneself to the church and community as a servant, rather than an employee.

Moving forward in his career took Harry from his church in the Lower Mainland of British Columbia and sent him to the province's interior. After 16 years, Harry took a position as the pastor of the Summit Drive Church in Kamloops, British Columbia. Harry describes stepping into a troubled administration and bringing with him a bright, new approach.

Harry relates that during his installation service, he recalls asking God, "Just make me a blessing here." And so it was—it didn't take long before he knew everyone in the congregation by their first name. Harry believes that these are the kinds of relationships that genuinely count when we can connect with the people we are tasked to lead and make them part of the team.

His approach was to make everyone feel important, not to overlook any who were part of his congregation. Making everyone feel important got noticed by the people and made a massive difference in the church—and soon, the attendance grew once again.

Today, it is fascinating and exciting to watch Harry address the crowd, somehow extending that all-inclusive feeling to everyone he ministers to.

There is tremendous value in making everyone feel important, he says.

Harry describes his leadership approach as being democratic, pace-setting, coaching, and affirmative. He avoids laissez-faire, autocratic, or command-and-control approaches. Working with his church board, he prefers the collaborative leadership style—inclusive and bringing value to all involved.

Let's look at a few key points of leadership that Harry takes advantage of in his position as his congregation leader.

When it comes to self-talk, Harry always talks to himself in the positive. "I repeat to myself what the Bible says that's true of me: I'm a child of the King; I have been called to a life of good works. I am always to be a servant if I want to be great in his Kingdom."

"I have often felt that there are many people far more qualified than I am. I have honestly felt that way," Harry describes when discussing his mindset. "I am not an intellect. I came to peace in my early 20s, knowing that I am only asked to do my best; that is my mindset. I work at not letting myself get caught up in the comparison trap; comparison is deadly."

Harry's philosophy in life is a simple one that perfectly matches his career and chosen path—that is to be a servant, be a blessing, and encourage everyone to be their best.

Harry points out the book *The Purpose Driven Life* by Rick Warren, summarizes where he finds his vision, and sets his goals over time. "I find I need to make a list for the day of the things I need to do so I can use my time well. It also gives me a sense of satisfaction at the end of the day to see what I have accomplished. It helps me to stay focused."

Trusting people to learn and, more importantly, understand where they are coming from is very important. Know and listen, so you do not initially write them off. "I have many friends today who initially did not seem like they were a fit."

When faced with challenging people in his life, Harry says it is time to treat them with a little extra grace. "Love the people who irritate you. It enlarges your heart. It takes patience and prayer—and it seems to always be worth it."

Change can be driven in life by offering one's support in many ways. For Harry, that comes through prayer. "I think you can be a change agent by really seeking to be an example, by praying for everyone by name," Harry opines.

To Harry, every person is an essential part of the community. His relationship-building approach is simple: there are no second-class members, and everyone is essential.

How you look reflects on you and who you are, Harry advises. "Looking sloppy gives that impression right away; looking professional gives that impression also."

Exercise is a big part of Harry's life, as it helps physically and improves one's mental state. "I always try to walk briskly, and when I go to a building, I always attempt to take the stairs if I can. Being overweight shows a lack of discipline, which carries forward in other things in life."

Decluttering one's life and space is key to success, Harry suggests, because it helps when you know just what in your life is important—and when your life has been filled with far too many unnecessary things.

Profanity and bad language are absolutely repulsive to Harry. There's no value in cursing, he says, and nobody should ever turn to such words to express themselves.

There's plenty of value in having a good sense of honor, Harry advises, though with a bit of a caveat. "Take God really seriously—but ourselves not so much." He suggests that an excellent way to understand his position is to watch the movie, *What About Bob?*, to get some perspective and direction on honor.

Finally, Harry offers up one more nugget of advice for those who want to build upon their leadership skills and knowledge.

"Be inclusive," he says. "Tell people what God is doing in their lives. Send flowers to those who are ill. Listen well. Say thank you as much as possible. Greet warmly all who enter your world."

Harry also offered a unique approach to relationship building—based on that biblical reading that he has done every day for most of his life. Here it is an acronym—sort of—for the word "relationships," Each letter is tied to a verse from Proverbs.[5]

- **R**emember to listen: He who answers before listening—that is his folly and shame (Proverbs 18:13).
- **E**nemies are to be loved: If your enemy is hungry, give him food to eat; if he is thirsty, give him water to drink. In doing this, you will heap burning coals on his head, and the Lord will reward you (Proverbs 25:21-22).
- **L**ove, always: Let love and faithfulness never leave you; bind them around your neck, write them on the tablet of your heart (Proverbs 3:3).
- **A**pologize when needed: He who conceals his sin does not prosper, but whoever confesses and renounces them finds mercy (Proverbs 28:13).

- **T**ruthful speech is much appreciated: An honest answer is like a kiss on the lips (Proverbs 24:26).
- **I**nvest in the lives of others, especially the poor: A generous man will prosper; whoever refreshes others will himself be refreshed (Proverbs 11:25).
- **O**verlooking offense: Whoever would foster love covers over an offense, but whoever repeats the matter separates close friends (Proverbs 17:9).
- **N**ever brag: Let another praise you and not your own mouth; someone else, and not your own lips (Proverbs 27:2).
- **S**peak words of encouragement: Anxiety weighs down the heart, but a kind word cheers it up (Proverbs 12:25).
- **H**old your tongue when it comes to gossip: A perverse person stirs up conflict, and a gossip separates close friends (Proverbs 16:28).
- **I**dentify with the emotional state of others: Like one who takes away a garment on a cold day, or like vinegar poured on a wound, is one who sings songs to a heavy heart (Proverbs 25:20)
- **P**rocrastination is to be avoided: Do not withhold good from those to whom it is due when it is in your power to act. Do not say to your neighbor, "Come back tomorrow, and I'll give it to you" when you already have it with you (Proverbs 3:27-28).
- **S**ecrets are to be kept: A gossip betrays a confidence, but a trustworthy man keeps a secret (Proverbs 11:13).

Harry Bicknell—Interview Insights

- A positive attitude is necessary and provides a building block for your relationships.

- Don't be caught in the compassion trap. You have skills to use, but you won't have them all.
- Being a servant is a key to leadership.
- Be inclusive; love even those people who at first seem irregular in your life.
- Difficult people need extra grace.
- Everyone is important and has value.
- Looking sloppy gives that impression right away; looking professional
- also gives that impression.
- Know what is important in your life. Don't make your life too full of unnecessary things.
- Have a sense of honor.

Relationships

By Robert J. Verbree

On Signal Hill today, I heard an old man say
you people mustn't be from here,
we're always in your way.
You people from the city, you're always in a hurry.
You miss the whales, the birds, the sky, the sea.
The wind blowing through your hair and all around your knees.
Did you see the Turs, the Gull, and Auk?
The blueberries, the mushrooms, and the hawk.
Well, here's another sign I see, which tells the story clear.
You don't look people in the eyes.
When you pass, it's just a sneer.
How come you've lost the ability to laugh and joke and love?
This wasn't the original plan.
From our Maker up above.
Relationships are where it's at
Important yes, they are.
In fact, without relationships, you're a very lonely star.
Without each other, life is drudgery and dull.
To know others intensely.
Is the piece that makes life full.

Chapter 7

RELATIONSHIPS, MENTORING, INVESTMENT, AND GRATITUDE

I f I think of myself and my lack of skill earlier in my life, I can understand how so many others are struggling in the same way that I did. That's why it's so important that we all need to continue our leadership journey and keep building and feeding that desire to learn more and grow.

In today's world, leadership could be described in this way: like a car rolling down the highway at 100 mph without a driver or with an inexperienced driver—it will surely crash.

But if you put a trained driver in the car's seat, it can be directed where you want it to go and get it there successfully.

An inexperienced driver climbing into the driver's seat of our hypothetical car is probably going to crash. At the same time, someone with experience, skill, and training who's ready to take the wheel can direct that car—and your organization—in the direction that it should go.

Relationships

Perhaps the most important piece of this whole strategy is your relationships. Relationships can add to or subtract from your stress level, and also affect your ability to stay calm in a stressful environment.

It's very accurate that if things aren't going well at home or things aren't going well at work, your stress level goes way up. When things are going well at home, at work, and you live a purpose-fulfilled life, generally things are going well.

As Harry Bicknell would suggest, I can turn to Proverbs for a good thought on this topic: "As a man thinketh in his heart, so is he."[6] To me, this says that the way you act at home is the way you will operate at work, the way you will operate at sports, and the way you will lead your team. In my opinion, you can't be dishonest and deceitful in your relationships because this will follow through at your workplace as well. You can't be one person in private and another person at work.

Let's look at a situation I witnessed. A work colleague and his wife divorced, which unfortunately set off a chain of events in his life. He had two sons from this marriage, and one of them was struggling with the breakup. While my colleague was dealing with this on an ongoing basis, doesn't it make sense that he would take some of its effects to work each day? Wouldn't that affect how he treated others and his work as well? Sure it would.

Friends or significant others fit in this equation as well. If you have just had a major disagreement with your significant other, that will undoubtedly affect your day, week, or month. However, if you're quick to get these differences resolved, things will smooth out. Remember: the same wind blows on us all—the wind of discouragement, the wind of change, and the winds of disagreement. No one is exempt.

It is how you deal with these things, not allowing them to define you, and learning the skills to move forward, that are important. Sometimes, you just have to unhook the wagon carrying those negative feelings and emotions and carry on.

It's that simple, really. At times, we have to agree to disagree. This is not a failure; in fact, so-called failures are successes turned inside out.

Your Colleagues

Our colleagues at work are kind of like family in a lot of ways. We spend a lot of our time with them, and the importance of getting along goes almost without saying.

As a leader, though, you need to position things right. First and foremost, you are the boss—and you need to act like the boss. Strong relationships with your team are essential, but you need to remember that you are the one in charge.

At the same time, know them well and recognize how their skills benefit your team.

One leader I worked with knew this skill very well. He was aware of all his employees, their families, their likes and dislikes, their birthdays—his knowledge of the team was very impressive.

Now, this story happened more than 40 years ago at this point—and I still remember it, so you know it's a good one.

I was relatively new on the job, maybe a year or so in. I was working hard to prove myself, which is a typical drive for new police officers. At the time, my efforts were focused on a very detailed investigation of a significant theft; tools were being stolen from the local mill. I was putting in many hours of overtime, and many of my own hours too. It was slow going, but I was making progress.

My boss was accommodating and complimentary of my efforts. At the time, I was looking forward to the coming weekend. I was going to drive from Vanderhoof, British Columbia, down to Vancouver to see my brother and my parents, who were visiting from Newfoundland. Oh, and did I mention that it was also my 23rd birthday?

This was a long weekend off for me—Thursday through Sunday—and you can imagine I was pretty excited about it. On Wednesday at noon, the boss called me back to the office. I was in the middle of things and very focused but made my way back. He called me into his office space and said, "Verbree, I know how hard you've been working, and I can see you will get the results you are after. I want you to leave now for Vancouver, take the afternoon off, go and visit your Mom and Dad, and enjoy your birthday together."

I was taken aback that he took the time to know all this information about me, and it was great. He gave me the afternoon off gratis, and his birthday wishes were also appreciated.

Let me tell you, if you think I wanted to do my absolute best for him when I got back to work that Monday, you are right. On the R-Y-G scale—this one definitely gets a Green!

Five People

There's a saying that goes around: you are the average of the five people you spend the most time with. I live by this and consider my relationships closely to make sure that my average doesn't drop!

Know who is in your room, and make sure you are around people who inspire you to be the best you can be—the people who light a fuse under you, those who light your fire.

I have a simple personal rule, no negative people in my life, and I promptly excuse myself if things start to become negative. And yes, for me, that has sometimes meant ending some friendships—the friends who seemed always to be negative or spent too much time merely sucking the life energy out of me.

Think of it this way. There are three kinds of people in your life. You have fruit producers, fruit pickers, and those from the past.

We like to spend our time around the fruit producers—that goes without saying, really. These are those people who inspire us or make us better human beings. Fruit pickers, well, they're the ones who just take and don't provide. So, keep those fruit producers in your life, and let the fruit pickers find someplace else to ply their trade.

Think about your life as if it was a room with one door. Should you let people in if they are not suitable for you? Nope. Try only to allow the people who can share something to help build you up.

What about those who are already in there or who have been able to sneak in? It's possible to shut them down and remove their negativity from your thinking—the best way I've found is to use the ho'opono-pono technique.

Never heard of it? Well, there's a heck of a lot more to it than I can share in this book, but the basics are simple. This is an ancient Hawaiian ritual that, when you break down the meaning, translates to "make it right" or "correct a mistake." There are four phrases that are the central part of this ritual: "I'm sorry," "forgive me," "I love you," and "I am grateful." Repentance, forgiveness, love, and gratitude. Name the person who's causing the problem, and repeat those phrases to yourself—it helps, believe me.

Be around those who make you a better person and let that aura spill over onto those you are with. You will be amazed at the difference that this will make in your stress-filled work environment. I know, I have done it.

Defining a Good Relationship

Several characteristics make up good, healthy working relationships. Let's look at them, and then I'd like you to take a moment to write down some thoughts on each of these points, all right?

Trust—This is the foundation of every good relationship. When you trust your team and colleagues, you form a powerful bond that helps you work and communicate more effectively. If you trust the people you work with, you can be open and honest in your thoughts and actions, and you don't have to waste time and energy "watching your back."

How can you develop more trust with your team?

Mutual Respect—When you respect the people you work with, you value their input and ideas, and they value yours. Working together, you can develop solutions based on your collective insight, wisdom, and creativity.

How can you develop more or better mutual respect?

Mindfulness—This means taking responsibility for your words and actions. Those who are mindful are careful and attend to what they say, and they don't let their own negative emotions impact the people around them.

How can you develop better mindfulness?

Welcoming Diversity—People with good relationships not only accept diverse people and opinions, but they also welcome them. For instance, when your friends and colleagues offer different views from yours, you take the time to consider what they have to say and factor their insights into your decision-making.

How can you best welcome diversity?

Open Communication—We communicate all day, whether we're sending emails and DMs or meeting face-to-face. The better and more effectively you communicate with those around you, the richer your relationships will be. All good relationships depend on open, honest communication.

How can you best promote open communication?

Mentoring

"If I have seen further than others, it is by standing on the shoulders of giants."

—Isaac Newton

Probably one of the top pieces to becoming a great leader is having a mentor. Most, if not all, successful business tycoons and leaders have an ongoing mentor. For instance, motivational author Jim Rohn was lucky to have entrepreneur and speaker Earl Schoff as his mentor. In turn, Rohn went on to mentor Tony Robbins and others.

If you genuinely want to grow, you need to be in the company of people who know more than you do, people who are successful and can help you reach success as well.

I have been lucky to have some great mentors in my life.

When I was attending technical school back in the 1970s, learning the trade of auto mechanics, I was placed under a man named Fred, who had worked in the trade for over 40 years. He was a true master, and one of his most extraordinary skills was that he understood the need to teach others to be as good as he was so that the trade would continue with successful professionals.

I just loved learning from him and being in his company. He was always patient with me and helped me master automotive repair.

One day I was working on a car that had electrical trouble. I had spent over an hour trying to find the issue. Fred patiently let me continue my efforts, although I could see in his eyes that he knew where the problem was. By the time an hour had passed, I was getting frustrated and not thinking clearly.

Fred came over and asked me if I was following the best procedure. I had to answer truthfully—no, I wasn't. He told me that following a system was the best practice—and that meant looking at the wiring diagram, following the flow chart to identify and find the problem, and narrowing down the causes. Following his advice, I went on to find the problem in a few minutes. This taught me several things: first, it is always a good idea to follow the procedure if you've got one to work from; and second, we all need a mentor.

Even today, I have a mentor to help me in a different business and keep me on track.

A great mentor helps you with things you can't read in a book or look at on a YouTube video. A good starting point is to understand that you cannot do everything yourself. You need to be in the company of people who know more than you do.

If you consider Fred's story above, it is possible to see some of the great qualities and attributes that great leaders have. Back to Proverbs for a moment: "In the multitude of counsellors there is safety." I genuinely believe this—the more people you can get on board with you, the more people who can share their wisdom and help guide you along, the better.

My mentor, Fred, knew things that were not readily available to me, and he could breathe these things into my experience from his experience. I do believe that experience does count for a large portion of value that many leaders miss.

Some Key Reasons Why Mentors Are Important

- **Mentors coach**: Mentors can coach and prepare you for change with their wise counsel and experience. Great leaders will have a desire to help you be successful from their own experience.

- **Mentors motivate**: Mentors can see outside of the forest you currently exist in and sharpen your focus and vision. They can provide ideas, thoughts, and insights that challenge and enable you to see beyond your current sphere of influence.

- **Mentors challenge**: Mentors encourage you to go further than you think you can. They push you to go farther than you see as being possible right now. A mentor pushes you beyond the borders of procrastination and fear and helps you understand what can be if you stick with it, with appropriate encouragement. A good mentor doesn't see failure; they see a way not to do it again and, in it, a great learning experience.

- **Mentors protect**: Mentors protect you from land mines and barriers that exist in many organizations and help you see a way around, over, under, or through. They teach you how to respond and not react to what can derail you. A mentor can use their sound counsel and experience to guide you through safely.

- **Mentors share life lessons from their experiences**: A good mentor has been where you are now and has learned from his or her previous experiences. Mentors use their stories and perspectives to show you what is possible. A great mentor never quits believing, encouraging, and engaging their student until their mission is a reality.

Let's engage your mind and explore mentoring—and how you, as a strong leader, can share your knowledge with those in your team. For each of the following, take some time and write out an answer exploring the question.

- Great mentors show interest in your success: How can you, as a leader, show interest in your employees' success or those under you?

- Great mentors are aligned with your best interest: How can you, as a leader, show that you are aligned with your employees' success or those under you?

- Great mentors focus on helping you be the best you can be: How can you, as a leader, show that you are helping your employees or those under you be the best they can be?

- Great mentors do not compete with you but rather complement you: How can you, as a leader, show that you complement your employees or those under you?

- Great mentors are not afraid of your successes or threatened by them: How can you, as a leader, show that you are not threatened by your employees' success or those under you?

- Do you have a mentor? It is certainly worth considering this. When some people are asked this question, they immediately say they cannot afford a mentor. My response would be that you can't afford not to have a mentor.

- If I think about the last five years of my life—and as I write this, I've just turned 63—the mentors I have been involved with have helped me grow immensely. I wouldn't be where I am today without their input.

Investment

An interesting principle says that you will receive an investment back many times over if you invest or give something. It is written that whatever a man sows, that he will also reap. Do you want good relationships? Invest in relationships. Do you want to be a great leader? Invest in leadership and master these skills.

Remember our analogy earlier of fruit producers and fruit pickers? Well, consider the producers to be the investors, and the pickers to be the takers. Investors, those who are givers by their nature, practice the principle of investment. The takers are the ones who don't see giving as an investment, and so they try to hoard whatever they have.

Ultimately, the investors win because they receive back many times over what they have invested. The takers ultimately lose because they lose disposition, friends, health, and respect. We have all seen the leader who isn't interested in helping—they want it all for themselves. At the end of the road, these people turn out to be miserable and gloomy. Conversely, the leader who invests in his people, the parents who invest in their family, and the person who invests in relationships, does receive a reward.

There's a book by Robert Gilmour LeTourneau called *Mover of Men and Mountains.*[7] It is an excellent read about investing in people and leadership. I highly encourage you to read it from cover to cover—it's that good.

LeTourneau was an interesting fellow. Born in Vermont in 1888, he received a Grade 7 education but went on to become an inventor of earthmoving machinery and built a massive business empire. In his day, his contemporaries referred to him as "God's businessman."

Christianity was important to LeTourneau—so important that he served both God and humanity by setting aside 90 percent of his salary and company profits for God, living on the other 10 percent.

He struggled hard in his early life and often found little abundance to be had, but he kept investing in others around him. A believer in practical instruction effectiveness combined with classroom learning, he bought a military hospital and land in Longview, Texas, in 1946. At that site, the LeTourneau Technical Institute was founded, offering up technical and mechanical training, college course offerings, and training for missionary technicians—all based on a philosophy that focused on work, education, and Christian learnings. In 1961, the technical institute became a college, and after that, LeTourneau University.

As for LeTourneau himself, he worked hard with the company, serving as president and board chairman from 1929 through 1966. Away from the upper floor offices, he was known as chief engineer and worked alongside his employees and engineers throughout his life. He could frequently be seen running equipment one minute and handling the corporate rigamarole the next, but it was always known that he preferred the former to the latter!

Many successful businesspeople rise to a rich and pampered life, but not LeTourneau. Instead, he wanted nothing more than to serve— spending his time at the drawing board with his engineers or walking the factory floor to connect with his employees.

This is an excellent example of someone willing to give back every moment of every day of his life. LeTourneau had the drive to invest in his people, and he was rewarded greatly for it.

I can't think of a single better example of investing in people and relationships than Robert Gilmour LeTourneau.

Gratitude

Gratitude is a distinctive characteristic of a person that shows wisdom, maturity, and humility. When leaders value gratitude, employees show their appreciation more readily.

This is true in your relationships and your home as well. Gratitude builds relationships.

It seems today that so many people are ungrateful. Most conversations I hear are negative and complaining. The weather is terrible, taxes are too high, and on and on it goes.

In positive psychology research, gratitude is strongly and consistently associated with greater happiness and a higher vibration. Gratitude helps people feel more positive emotions, relish good experiences, improve their health, deal with adversity, and build strong relationships.

In the Bible, 1 Thessalonians 5:16-18 states: "Rejoice always, pray without ceasing, give thanks in all circumstances."[8] Gratitude is defined as the state of being grateful—thankfulness.

I believe in this so strongly that I have a gratitude journal that I write in every day. It does make all the difference. People who practice gratitude consistently report a host of benefits.

Physically, they often have a more robust immune system and are less bothered by aches and pains; they have lower blood pressure, tend to exercise more, and take better care of their health; and they sleep longer and feel refreshed upon waking.

Psychologically, grateful people have higher levels of positive emotions. They're more alert, alive and awake, feel more joy and pleasure, and express more optimism and happiness.

These people are more helpful, generous, and compassionate; they are more forgiving, more outgoing, and less lonely and isolated.

During my law enforcement career, I had a clerk working for me who was always negative and complaining. Her gratitude meter was low.

She was always complaining about how others left her out, her husband didn't care, her kids were disrespectful, her workload was too great, and other ladies in the office were excluding her. She could be so negative that she could suck the juice out of a carrot.

One day she asked to talk to me. She started complaining about her workload, her lunch break being too short, problems with the other ladies in the office, how she hated her job, and on…and on!

I asked her why she hated her job, and she went off like a wide-open fire hose. I let her go for a while. After her rant wrapped up, I asked her if there was anything she liked about her job, and she said no—she hated her job, and she hated everything about it.

I asked a simple question: "Do they pay you for coming to work?" Of course, she said they did—she had to have a paycheck, and she had earned it. I said, "Don't you like getting paid?"

She looked at me strangely, as if it was her right to get paid. "So," I said, "there is one thing you do like about your job. I am sure there are more."

I impressed upon her that she should write out a list of things that she was thankful for every day and say them out loud first thing in the morning and the last thing at night before she went to bed.

This didn't impress her much, to be honest, but she did tell me she would try. I had little hope, and there didn't seem to be much of a change for a long time. But as time progressed, she did change from a faultfinder to a good finder, and it was most interesting to see the changes that came about. She was generally happier at her job, the ladies at the office began to include her in their activities, and there were some positive changes in her home life.

Gratitude is enormous, and it should not be overlooked. It is a big piece of the leadership puzzle.

Gratitude

By Robert J. Verbree

Sitting in a hotel room while away on vacation,
In a category one hurricane,
The power goes out, soon anticipation.
At first, it's crazy with laughter and fun,
We light the place up with our cell phones on.
Soon joking and smart remarks abound,
Stories from childhood come to our minds.
We have lots of food and drink,
But after an hour, it gets kind of down.
No phone, no Internet, TV or radio, no heating or cooling, a very cold
   shower,
It's not like the power will be on in an hour.
The wind is blowing a gale, and the rain is spilling in bucketloads.
Very soon, we recognize the blessing of hydro,
Without it, just about everything is a no go.
Do we take things for granted, does our attitude stink?
There are many alive who don't have even a sink, not the bare neces-
   sities of living,
While we banter on about this little misgiving.
I want to change my ways, I boldly assert to myself,
Being grateful is a piece of the life puzzle.
It's hard to change my ways, a really big struggle,
I'm committed to changing it up.
Help me, my Maker, with all of this stuff.

It can be done say the best of the best,
Different thinking and values must come from the chest.

Chapter 8

LEADERSHIP IN MANY DIFFERING ENVIRONMENTS

Toomas Ruberg

I n 1948, a pair of refugees from Estonia who had settled in Sweden welcomed a son. Toomas Ruberg's life started out rather unusually, thanks to his surroundings. Still, as he negotiated life with his family as an immigrant to Canada and a long career in the Canadian Armed Forces, he became a leader whose skills and knowledge are an excellent example to follow.

Toomas and his family lived in Sweden for four years, but that time came to an end abruptly due to his father's unique occupation.

"My father was actually working for MI-6, the Secret Intelligence Service in the United Kingdom—he was a spy, and he went back into Russia after the war," Toomas relates. "One day, he came home and said the Russians had found out he had a family in Sweden, and it was time to leave."

The Rubergs were whisked out of Stockholm to London, where they spent six months before Toomas' father was offered the opportunity by the British government to go anywhere within the Commonwealth. He chose Canada, and they were off, settling in Montreal in 1952.

It was challenging to settle into the Canadian landscape, but Toomas says his parents were both skilled and found roles quickly.

"My father was an artist and very eccentric, and my mother was very talented—she spoke six languages, and she had been a teacher in Estonia," he remembers.

Life for the Rubergs was often stringent, thanks to Toomas' father's views—he had very strong morals and rules for the family.

"He was very nationalistic, and he hated the Russians with a passion…we had to go to church every Sunday, and then to Estonian school after church. I learned to read and write Estonian—it's not the simplest language to learn," Toomas says. "My brother and I had to speak Estonian at home—we were not allowed to speak English."

As Toomas moved through school, he decided that he wanted to become an engineer and took advantage of his adopted country's opportunities to get there—by joining the Navy.

"I thought, *If someone is willing to pay me to go to university, this is a pretty good deal!*" he says. "So, I joined the Royal Canadian Navy—at the time, it was a good experience. I got to go to sea every summer, and I got to see parts of the world I would not have seen otherwise."

As his engineering education at McGill University wound down, Toomas applied for an Athlone Fellowship, a prestigious program offered to top engineering graduates in Canada. The fellowship included two years of postgraduate study at top universities in the United Kingdom.

Toomas was awarded the fellowship, took some leave from his military career, and spent three years at Cambridge University, where he completed his doctorate in metallurgy.

Then the Canadian Forces came calling again, and Toomas wound up swapping over to the Air Force, eventually ending up in Cold Lake, Alberta, where his new skills were quickly put to work.

"I went to the aerospace test facility in Cold Lake—this was an excellent experience in the aircraft structures department. I was also in charge of the drafting department there, which was a unionized department," he remembers.

Cold Lake was where Toomas started to shape his leadership skills, although it's hard to get away from a style that fits the basics when it comes to the military.

"My leadership style was command and control at this time. That's what the military works on, and the military is a separate society. Everyone knows where they stand and what's expected of you, and as long as you follow their rules, you're fine," he says. "Command and control were a little bit tough in the drafting department. They had their union rep who would contest anything. So, if you wanted to change anything, you had to document everything, a very long process to make changes."

After establishing himself and his skills at Cold Lake, Toomas moved up the officers' ranks in the Canadian Armed Forces, reaching major, and was sent to Europe for some years, where he met his wife. After that, it was back to Ottawa, where he was a player in developing the CF-18 fighter before he was sent to Staff College in Toronto for more training.

Command was waiting for Toomas as he advanced, and he found himself the detachment commander for quality assurance in the Toronto area, he explained.

"I looked after all the Air Force contracts for the Toronto area and had about a dozen people working for me at the time. They were all public servants, so once again, I had to deal with the union situation... it's not easy to switch from the command-and-control approach which I used in Germany, where you know that if you tell someone to do something and they disobeyed, there were severe repercussions."

After working in Toronto, Toomas moved to Ottawa, receiving a promotion to Lieutenant Colonel in the process, and taking over as the director of engineering and maintenance for Canadian fighters and trainers. Then there was a stint at the NATO supreme headquarters in Belgium, followed by time in Germany with Canada's premiere maintenance squadron.

Germany proved to be an eventful place to be during Toomas' stint—small things occurred, like the fall of the Berlin Wall and the first Gulf War, which Canada participated in from its German bases.

Eventually, the base closed in 1993, and Toomas returned to Canada having been its last commanding officer—and then became the commanding officer of the aerospace development unit in Trenton, Ontario, before finally retiring in 1995.

As a military man, Toomas relied on command and control as his leadership approach because that's how the military tends to do it. But, finding himself in the private sector, he found it was time to rethink his approach—especially as he stepped into new industries and situations.

He took his first step in Kamloops, British Columbia, where he signed on with Weyerhaeuser at its sawmill as reliability systems leader.

"I had to switch my management style considerably—I had to become a collaborative manager. Now, everything was by influence—not by order," he relates. "That was tough because first of all, I was a newcomer to the forest industry. I had all these old guys who had worked in a sawmill for 20 years. They regarded me with a bit of suspicion."

At the time, Weyerhaeuser had 13 mills across Canada. Toomas found that his efforts could provide strong supports across the mill network—even small projects like creating a select group of saw filers, who had a significant influence on the quality of the lumber being produced. However, there were challenges to be faced.

"The toughest time I had was with the mill managers—they were pretty dyed-in-the-wool guys, and there was a varying reception to change," he says. "The mills that didn't change eventually closed."

Once established with Weyerhaeuser, Toomas saw duty at various mills and in multiple positions—operations manager, capital projects manager, and others. One-stop was a little more unique and challenging.

"I did a stint in Claresholm, Alberta, as the plant manager for Weyerhaeuser Trus Joist®—that was quite interesting. They put me in there to close the plant, which was not an easy position to be put in," he recalls.

Today, Toomas operates his own consulting company, continuing to provide leadership to those in various industries.

The leadership skills and knowledge that Toomas has built up over his years in the military and industry have provided many valuable insights. Let's take a look at a few of these.

Firstly, Toomas advises, "Don't panic. It makes the troops nervous," he says.

When it comes to self-talk, Toomas says he always wants to remain upbeat and positive. This has guided him through his many different roles in the private sector, whether it was with the sawmills, working in the mining industry or his own consulting business, and providing course material for educational institutes.

His mindset and philosophy in life are quite simple: everyone should serve themselves rather than rely on others. "I get very upset with people who think they are very entitled to everything—that is very irritating to me," he says. "I don't believe anyone should be starving or left out in the cold, but at the same time, I don't think they should be given everything on a silver platter. There is a balance there, and I don't think our society has achieved that."

Family and local society are at the top of Toomas' list in his philosophy. He is a very proud Canadian who helps where he can and feels terrible for Canadians who have a hard time.

A good leader's vision should be to assist their team when necessary but not to be afraid to bring up problems. "Always support your subordinates when they are in the right, and never fail to correct them when they are in the wrong. I applied this in all my management positions," he advises. "You can't allow things to deteriorate—you have to keep in mind that the longer you don't do something, if something is going wrong, then the worse it's going to get. It won't get better on its own. Having the inner strength to take those things on is very important."

As a leader, it's also good form to remember that while you can be friendly with the people you are over, you cannot be friends with them— as Toomas notes, the saying, "It's lonely at the top," is very true.

"It's important always to listen—and think—before you speak," he says, "and while delegation of work and trusting your people to do their work is a good approach, don't forget to keep that supervision up. I do believe that you do have to monitor their progress—you have to make sure that things are on track," Toomas says. "The odd time, you have to apply a course correction if you see things veering one way or another."

Both his military and civilian employers helped Toomas out with various training types that expanded his leadership skills. "Weyerhaeuser, for example, sponsored me for my MBA degree," he notes. "They were quite a progressive company—I did a lot of training for them as well, on reliability and maintenance, and likewise with the mining industry. I received excellent training in both the civilian industries and the military."

Difficult people are everywhere and in every kind of role, but there are situations in which they're more challenging to deal with.

"In the command-and-control environment, it was probably easier to deal with them. This is because you, as the leader, had the ultimate authority. You could order your people to do it, and they had no other choice other than to quit. In the end, you had the hammer; you could tell them, 'I have listened to you, but this is what I want to be done,'" he relates.

"The civilian world was more challenging, especially in environments where unions were involved," Toomas says. "There, you had to work harder to provide reasoning for any disputed decisions when it came to difficult employees. They would have the union shop steward there, and it would go back and forth. You would have to state your reasons very firmly, and you would also have to have documentation about why you were doing whatever you were doing. There were so many last chances that were given to people in the union environment. That can be very frustrating."

When it comes to being the change, Toomas advocates humility and trust—show your people that you trust them and use that to establish your relationships with your team. He also encourages small steps rather than one giant leap to make changes.

It's hard not to dress for success in a military environment because if you don't, a drill sergeant will remind you—usually at high volume! For Toomas, that habit—which, in his Canadian Armed Forces years meant he pressed his shirts because his wife's ironing never quite met the needs—has carried over into civilian life.

"I never wore jeans. I always wore a shirt when I went into a mill; I never wore a T-shirt," he says. "Dress appropriately and not sloppily."

Exercise has been a lifelong thing for Toomas, likely again a hold-over from military life. "I exercise every day—I may be a little overboard here…exercise is the best release for stress and all kinds of other things associated with a busy job."

Toomas admits that he's a little more cluttered than some success-ful leaders might find comfortable. "I am probably overcluttered—I've stopped worrying about it. I'm still working on this aspect of my life. Like most, I have too much stuff."

It's not a good idea to let your language get rowdy around Toomas—bad language is a pet peeve. "I don't like it when people use the F-word perpetually, where every third word is the F-word—it even bothers me in the gym when I go there. I don't see the need for it, and I don't under-stand why people have to do that; it doesn't bring any value. It detracts," Toomas says. "So much music these days is like that too; I don't like it. Vocabulary is directly related to behavior."

Honor is something Toomas is still working on—he admits that sometimes it's hard to understand when he's trying to be funny. "I have a sense of honor that is a little sarcastic sometimes—not everyone gets my honor, but honor is very important," he says.

Toomas Ruberg—Interview Insights

- Command and control can work in the military but don't nec-essarily fit in civilian life.
- Always support your subordinates when they are in the right, and never fail to correct them when they are in the wrong.

- It's important always to listen—and think—before you speak.
- Checking on employee progress is positive, done in the right way.

Chapter 9

YOUR LEVEL OF INFLUENCE, NOT YOUR LEVEL OF AUTHORITY:

Vision, Mission, and Goals

To this point, we have learned about the importance of making decisions, our self-talk, and our mindset. You should have implemented or hopefully are working on implementing some of these tips already. Some changes can be almost immediate and very short-term, while others will take a little more time.

It's vital that, as we work through these changes and improvements in your leadership skills, we understand the core pieces—the anchors of what leadership looks like. In this chapter, those anchor pieces focus on your influence and how influence does not necessarily equate to authority. Let's talk about your vision, your mission, and your goals.

Today when I was out walking, I was enjoying nature. The sunshine's warmth and the fact that it's springtime were amazing to me. I was very grateful for the new growth I could see all around me. It was fantastic to see the fresh, green buds bursting forth on the trees, signalling a new beginning.

A new beginning—that's kind of what this book is all about, right? Our leadership journey is about new beginnings in our leadership style.

People use their leadership skills every day. Earlier today, when I went to a government office to renew an official document, a man outside was screening people who went inside. His manner was concise and very curt—very command and control. That ruffled my feathers, and almost instantly, I had my back up. He didn't need to act like this; he just wanted to be in control. Everyone in the line felt just the same way.

Inside, the person that I dealt with moments later at the service counter was totally different. This person was inclusive with a great demeanour, and it was a pleasure to be in his company. What a difference just two minutes apart and two personalities make when it comes to two different leadership styles. Remember: we use the skills of leadership and sales every day.

As I reflect on my 35 years in the policing world, I am reminded about the good leaders I worked for and the bad ones I worked for. Sad to say that it seems like I worked for more bad ones than good ones—or, perhaps it's better described as more untrained ones than good ones. My son had a similar military experience, and my son-in-law experienced abysmal leadership in private industry.

I want to move forward and teach you that leadership is your level of influence and not your level of authority.

Leadership potential exists within each of us. That potential can be triggered by outside events or by exploring great ways to lead adopted from others who have done it successfully.

Once you learn your "superpower" of leadership, you will be able to build the confidence it takes to lead and influence. We have all heard the saying, "Leaders are born, not made." While it is true that some people are born leaders, most leaders are forged in the flames of adversity.

I can certainly resonate with that. It is interesting, as long as there have been leaders, other people have been trying to determine how those leaders were, or are, successful.

It is essential to understand in today's world that leadership is not about title, level, or office. The best leaders we find today can be great followers and great influencers as well.

Tim's Story

A very close friend of mine, Tim, is an elementary school principal. He has been in the teaching profession for nearly three-and-a-half decades, and he is good at his job.

Tim is a great leader with a great demeanour. He is an influencer. He works in a high-stress environment and has to keep so many balls in the air; it's crazy to try and comprehend.

Even with all the stress and challenges, he works very hard at being a great leader—and it shows. His employees love him and would go to war with him. How does he do it? Well, knowledge, for one. He knows about each of them and takes care to acknowledge their birthdays and to be aware of problems in their lives. He does his best to build and support them and to say "yes" whenever he can. Tim is very inclusive and is willing to follow when someone on the team knows more than he does.

Team building is a big part of leadership, and Tim's always quick to take advantage of opportunities.

For example, Anne, one of his team members, recently had a significant moment come up—her son was playing in a hockey game that could mean his shot at being selected to the NHL. This was a big deal—and Tim understood completely.

Secretly, he arranged for each worker at his school to be at the game to support Anne and her son. Anne and her family were completely surprised by the arrival of her co-workers at the game! But, more than this, imagine the strength that such a simple act forged in the work environment. It's hard to describe just how much of an impact this kind of thing has when a leader provides this kind of support.

Tim performs this kind of activity for all his employees, and he is good at it, but it has taken much learning on his behalf to get to this point.

Recently, Tim let it slip that he was considering retiring soon. Can you imagine what a fuss that caused? The superintendent of schools dropped by to see Tim personally and asked him to reconsider—that's quite a statement on his reputation and abilities!

You can almost sum up Tim's job worldview this way: look for opportunities, have fun at work, and make it so much fun you would do it for free (although the pay is excellent!). This doesn't say there will not be bad days and challenges, but overall, make it enjoyable to be at work. When people see you having fun and enjoying your work, they will tend to have fun and enjoy their work.

Tim fully understands the concept of the level of influence, not the level of authority. Just like all of us as leaders, there are times when Tim must take control, but even in those times, his team understands that he has their backs and, when that situation arises, they are all willing to listen and contribute at that level.

This is one of the key points I want to get across in this chapter: influence is better than being authoritative; and having a clear vision, mission, and goals are also essential.

Leadership in the digital age should not be telling others what to do, as the command-and-control model calls for. Leadership in the 21st century should be focused on inspiring and influencing your people to do what needs to be done, listening to their ideas, getting them all the tools they need, and being happy and complimentary about the outcome.

A title alone does not make you a leader. Genuine leaders can take a stand and motivate others to join them in the journey—this is called vision, which we'll get to in a moment. It is through the skills of influence that leadership works best.

But Bob, you might ask, what about taking over in a caustic work environment? What about a house full of unruly teenagers? What about at that volunteer job when direction is lacking? What about consulting work, where you are challenged openly?

This is where mission, vision, and values fit. They are a starting point.

Vision: Creating Clear Direction

"Where there is no vision, the people perish." That's another quality point made in Proverbs.

Leadership begins with a vision. A leader without a dream has a problem right out of the gate. A vision is a clear picture of where and what the leader sees his people or group going or doing. The vision must be understood and promoted by the leader and accurately explained and understood by the employees or group.

In short, the vision is the driving force behind your leadership.

Your commitment to act on this is called the mission. The measurable steps to achieve the mission are called goals.

The leader must have one vision, one mission, and many goals to get where he is going.

Here's a story from a friend of mine and how he used his vision, mission, and goals to succeed.

Max was newly promoted as the company's transportation manager with more than 200 trucks in Edmonton, Alberta. He took over the job from a person who had held the position for more than 30 years. Everything was running fine, but there were many inefficiencies too.

For the previous few years, this manager had kept a low profile, not wanting to rock the boat with retirement drawing near. Max had a vision to streamline the operation, make it more efficient, and save money. His new mission met with some of the other senior managers' resistance, who thought it was too aggressive.

Max typed out his vision on a 3x5 card and had it laminated. Then, he put this card in a frame in a prominent place on his desk to see it and envision it continuously. By doing this, he had the drive to act every day. He was reminded of his vision every time he looked at that card.

Next, he wrote out his department's mission statement and made sure that it aligned with the company mission statement. Then he wrote out his goals in measurable steps on separate pages in his notebook: where he wanted to be in six months, a year, 18 months, and 24 months. He allowed for corrections and new and better ideas along the way and avoided overcomplicating the process.

His next step was to meet with and communicate these goals and time frames to his employees, starting with the assistant managers and then following up with his entire team.

There was, of course, pushback because change always seems to be met with resistance, but his resolve was firm, and he brought plenty of experience to the job. He told his employees his door was always open and that he would like to hear their ideas and suggestions.

Max made a point of going out onto the floor daily, talking to his people and getting to know them. Soon a bond of trust was forming, and great ideas were being shared. It was clear that the vision Max had was heady. Still, in very little time, everyone had taken ownership of their part of the project—and it was all because of the trust Max put in his people, as well as his willingness to listen to everyone—from the newest employee to the most senior.

With Max's story in mind, here's an exercise. Let's write out our vision statement. Remember, a vision is a clear picture of where and what the leader sees his people or group going or doing.

Six Things to Think About as You Do This

- Project one to five years into the future.
- Determine your purpose and position as an organization.
- Describe what success looks like in your operations.
- Consider your company type and structure.
- Reference your competitors or create an analogy.
- Describe a measurable goal.

As an example, here is my vision for what you're reading right now—and beyond:

I want to develop and create a how-to book and an online course that is different from what currently exists, that will be easy to understand with usable steps that can be implemented daily within the next one to three years.

Write out your vision, and ask yourself: Does it pass the R-Y-G test?

Mission Statements

The commitment to act is called the mission. Highly effective leaders tend to be goal-oriented, and as such, they frequently have both a personal mission statement and a work-based mission statement. They understand where they are going and why.

You must first have a strong foundation on which you build your goals. A mission statement is designed to help you set goals that will drive change in your personal life and your organization.

To do that, you must first understand what drives you—your principles and values. Principles and values are fundamental truths about ourselves and our ideas; they are the fabric of who we are. Principles are things like fairness, honesty, and integrity. Values are beliefs and opinions that we hold regarding specific issues or ideas, expressing our personal views and opinions. These often help us accomplish objectives based on our current circumstances.

Mission statements can be made for any type of organization. Everyone in the organization should develop organizational mission statements. If there is no involvement in the process, there will be no commitment to the idea.

An organization may have an all-encompassing mission statement; even each team may have their own. However, they should all dovetail with each other.

As an exercise to help you understand this point, let's complete a mission statement together. Write this down in your notebook.

Describe What Your Company Does: What product or service does your business produce or provide?

Describe How Your Company Does What It Does: List the core values essential to express in your business.

Add Why Your Company Does What It Does: This is the part of your mission statement that describes your spark—the passion behind your business.

Put Your New Mission Statement to Work: Once you've crafted your business's new mission statement, you'll want to put it to work right away.

How did that work out for you? To compare, here is my mission statement:

To provide superior training, be a great teacher, and inspire leaders to be more than they thought they could be.

There are many great examples of mission statements to be found—if you take time to google mission statements, you'll find the mission statements of many great leaders. It's quite fascinating, and I would encourage you to take the time to craft a personal mission statement and your work mission statement.

How does your mission statement do when you put it up against the R-Y-G test?

Goal Setting

We've ticked off vision and mission statements, so that leads us to goals. What are they, and why are they important?

Goals are specific, close-ended, quantifiable objectives with a fixed time frame for achieving them. To encourage your success, make goal setting an ongoing practice.

Setting goals at work is an intriguing balancing act. On the one hand, your workplace goals must support the company mission; but on the other hand, they must be your own. Otherwise, goal setting is just a mechanical, check-the-box exercise.

An additional complication is that some companies (and managers) are better at helping their employees set and achieve work goals than others. The good news is that even if you work for someone who approaches the annual goal-setting session as a necessary evil, there are things you can do to get some value out of it. Suppose your manager genuinely understands the power of goal alignment and setting and achieving goals. In that case, you have an excellent opportunity to use the conversation as a starting point for career growth.

10 Things to Keep in Mind Before Setting Goals at Work and Filling Out a Goal Sheet

- Know your group's structure.
- Discuss your mission statement with your boss, family, or volunteer group.
- Focus on and decide what you can and can't control.
- Think about your leadership growth in the long term.
- Think beyond immediate tasks and examine the big picture.
- Get clarity on what goal achievement would look like.
- Schedule periodic check-ins.
- Ask for support if you need it.
- Make a systematic comparison of your annual goals with your to-do list.
- Track your accomplishments.

Remember that setting goals for work is best when it is an ongoing practice. Please do yourself a favor and treat it as a conversation that never stops.

Every time you get a new assignment, ask your group to clarify expectations. What do they hope to accomplish through your work? Where do they anticipate difficulties? What is the timeline, and why is this project important?

After the project is wrapped up, have a conversation to debrief and talk about what went well and what could have been done better. Many leaders are apprehensive of performance discussions, but the truth is that you can only get better if you know what skills and habits need more work.

Keep the communication lines open, and you will set yourself up for more interesting work and a faster career progression in no time.

SMART Goal Setting

A widespread goal-setting program is the S-M-A-R-T action plan.

This stands for **Specific, Measurable, Attainable, Realistic, and Tangible**.

- Each goal must be a specific step.
- Each goal must be measurable, in terms of what is accomplished and also when it is accomplished.
- Each goal must be attainable.
- Each goal must be realistic.
- Each goal must be tangible.

Let's check back in with Max, shall we, and see how he is doing. Remember, Max had the vision to streamline the trucking operation where he worked as the transportation manager. He knows what his vision is. Remember it is on a 3x5 card on his desk. He uses the S-M-A-R-T program to write out his action steps or goals—and here they are.

My Goals for the First Six Months:

Specific steps:

- Standardize our parts—buy from one supplier if possible.
- Oil and filter.
- Brake parts.
- Tires.
- Hardware.
- Electrical parts.

- Wiper blades and windshield washer.
- Glass.

Measurable Results:

- Is this Attainable—YES or NO.
- Is this Realistic—YES or NO.
- Is this Tangible—YES or NO.

My Goals for the First 12 Months:

Specific steps:

- Standardize our fleet—buy or lease one brand of truck.
- Standardization of training.
- One line of parts to keep in stock.
- One electronic shop manual.
- Knowledge of one model.
- Less warranty hassles

Measurable Results:

- Is this Attainable—YES or NO.
- Is this Realistic—YES or NO.
- Is this Tangible—YES or NO.

As you can see, his plan was simple but effective. You can write out your plan in a similar way. It is a must to write your goals out and review them often.

In a Hurry

By Robert J. Verbree

Out on the highway.
Just bootin' along.
XM radio playin'.
I'm singin' along.
The highway is clear.
And the sky is dark gray.
Nothing impeding us
To keep on our way.
I look in the rearview.
A blue bullet approaches.
Its driver it seems
Is really ferocious.
At once, he is less than a car length behind.
This guy looks like he is out of his mind.
He's waving his hands.
Crossing over the line.
Wow, this guy is nuts.
Clear road he must find.
As soon as he can, he blows by like a shot.
He gives me the finger as he passes my yacht.
I ignore his advances and maintain my driving.
Soon he's a dot on the highway horizon.
Minutes later, at a traffic light.
Well, wouldn't you know it, the blue bullet's insight.
In fact, he is stopped in a long line of traffic.

One has to wonder why he was so frantic.

He won't look over as I stop by his car.

He stares straight ahead.

This silly nut bar.

Wow, today, it seems like the masses.

Are angry, impatient, and ready for clashes.

In a world of production, multitasking, and focus.

It seems like we're all so ready to blow up.

What is your philosophy of life, I must ask?

Is it hurry up, go faster, and look out for me?

Or is one of service, and humility

At the end of the day, does more hurry matter?

You can't take it with you.

In fact, it's the latter.

We arrive here with nothing.

And that's how we'll leave.

Do you think this will change

Which ego will we feed?

Chapter 10

YOU DON'T HAVE TO HAVE A BOOK IN FRONT OF YOU TO LEARN SOMETHING

Clara R. Norgaard

Today, in her 80s, the leadership knowledge and qualities of Clara Norgaard are immediately evident. She is an excellent example of a leader who has also broken new ground in her career—as one of the first women of color to serve as a mayor.

Clara was born in Edmonton, Alberta, in 1937, and spent her early life and schooling there before her family travelled west into British Columbia looking for business opportunities in 1956. On the way back from Prince George, they stopped in the small town of Clinton and wound up purchasing a piece of property, where they relocated to shortly afterwards. Her parents opened a plumbing shop, and Clara ventured out into business for the first time on her own, opening a ladies' clothing store.

In 1958, Clara sold her business in Clinton and followed her parents to the south central British Columbia community of Merritt. In 1960 Clara began dating Henry Norgaard, a customer she had met previously in her father's plumbing shop in Clinton. Henry had started a ready-mix plant in Merritt to provide concrete for the construction of Craigmont Mines and new housing developments being built in the growing community. The next year, on February 25, 1961, the two married.

Clara was involved in the concrete business for a big part of her life. Henry ran the operation, and Clara, as she said, "found the money." They were a strong team and together had a life philosophy that said, simply, you can do anything you put your mind to. Clara is quick to point out that you don't have to have a book in front of you to learn something.

"You have to enjoy your own company," Clara says when discussing how to live a happy, fulfilled life. The things in life that matter most to her are contentment with herself, family, friends, community, and her home. Material things can give illusions of happiness, but the spiritual things are what really count. Challenges have always been exciting for Clara. There are no mistakes or failures in life, only lessons to be learned. "If you aim for the stars and you get halfway there and reach your goal, be grateful."

Clara could always count on her parents. Her father was always willing to give her good advice and be her mentor, but he would not interfere in her life. Clara learned a lot about leadership growing up in her home and gained the value and philosophy that a little hard work never hurt anyone. It was up to her to put her father's advice to use or not. Both of her parents taught her to respect other people how she wanted to be respected and never compromise her integrity or beliefs.

Growing up, politics was always discussed at the dinner table. During the 1970s, she was involved in the Social Credit Party as president of the Yale-Lillooet Riding. In 1985 and 1986, Clara served as an alderman, and from 1991 to 1999, she was the mayor of Merritt, British Columbia. She was elected for three consecutive terms as mayor. This is the greatest accomplishment and area of personal pride for Clara.

The first three years as mayor were the most difficult, as there were three members of council who could not adjust to changes and move forward in a growth period. Some felt the mayor should be a man, which caused some serious concerns.

"The respect the people of my community have shown me is the greatest gift I have ever received," she says with pride.

It makes her smile when she sees people being kind to each other, young children having fun, and making dinner for family and friends. In her spare time, Clara enjoys knitting, reading, sewing, and gardening. "I like to read books that help to improve one's self, mentally and physically," she says.

Being raised to see people by their qualities, integrity, and respect for themselves and others is why she feels intolerance is the single most offensive act one human being can commit against another regularly.

Clara was taught to see others based on honesty, kindness, loyalty, and commitment—not their physical appearance, their economic status, or by the association of what they can do for you.

Greed and envy are the two worst cardinal sins, for Clara feels they make people unhappy all the time, not trustworthy, and dishonest. These characteristics alienate people from the rest of society and will make them lonely and bitter. The sins that follow are lust, gluttony, anger, pride, and sloth.

The meaning of life for her is to try and make the world a better place to live, and to do no harm to her fellow man. Clara believes, "One must make a commitment to the relationship, communication, respect, compassion, trust, and being there when the other person is feeling down."

Canada does not have one finest hour but many, according to Clara. It is the many times that Canada has stepped forward to help people in other countries in their time of need that makes it a great nation. Power, greed, and the excessive use of credit all contribute to what Clara feels is wrong with the world today.

"Some countries are trying to be the most powerful nations and will go to any length to achieve that desire. People around the world are very greedy and want power and money, and they will go to any length to achieve that desire, and in the industrialized countries, it is too easy to live on credit." Clara thinks the world is in chaos because of that excessive credit.

If she could regulate credit, she would make the rules more stringent so it would be harder to get. "People would have to live within their means and have fewer toys and unnecessary material things." She says, "We are here to propagate the human race, to try and promote peace with our fellow man, and to leave the world a better place to live when we die." She believes there is a God, but she does not practice any one religion. The Golden Rule, "Do unto others as you would have them do unto you," are words Clara lives by.

All the dreams that mattered did come true. She has a good marriage, family, friends, and success. Looking back on all aspects of her life, Clara says the only thing she would have invested more into if she knew then what she knows now would have been spending more time with family and friends. Clara's parents and grandparents lived into their 80s and late 90s, and she feels that her longevity has come partly from the genetics they shared with her—but that a large part of it comes from within each and every person. "I believe that if one thinks they are old, then they become old before their time. I have a philosophy that I want to be over 100—just to annoy my children," she jokes. "I enjoy life and hopefully will continue to do so for a very long time."

"I did my best to raise a good family, was faithful to my husband, whom I loved very much, faithful to my friends, and offered a helping hand when I could." These are words that would make her feel she lived a life to be proud of.

When it comes to leadership, Clara focuses on holding people working for her accountable—she believes in them and will coach them as needed. Being authoritative at times is necessary, but for the most part, she avoids micromanaging and is democratic. "You can talk to people and say, 'We have got to do this; now, how are we going to do it?' " she advises. "When people would say, 'It can't be done,' I would say, 'Yes, it can be done if you put your mind to it.' "

Connecting with your people is an integral part of ensuring that they thrive, and showing drive and passion for the job gets things done. There's always a way around the roadblocks that come up, Clara believes.

Staying positive and providing inspiration to your team to achieve their goals and accept the accolades—even when it was your idea—helps build camaraderie in your team and brings the best out of everyone. It also helps to encourage your people to ask for help when it's necessary.

When it comes to self-talk, Clara often focuses on thinking about what she might do in certain positions and how she would respond to different situations. "Talk to yourself in a positive way and ask what you should do."

Her mindset is very positive; she says that anything is possible and works hard to inspire others to move forward. That ties into her life philosophy and focuses on doing the right things at the right time. "Don't take yourself too seriously—no one is getting out of here alive. Remember that there's always a way around."

Hard work never hurt anyone, Clara believes, so her vision, mission, and goals are targeted on moving past asking why something can't be done and goes straight to getting out there to find a way to succeed. "Inspire loyalty, and be loyal to your team," she advises. Always do your homework to know what's going on and listen to your team. Offer up support when it's needed.

When it comes to being the change, Clara advocates bravery and trust as the keys. "Be brave enough to do and say the hard things—you don't do yourself any good if you keep that going. Just go do it." Believe in your people and their abilities, and coach them to provide guidance when they need it. Also, always work with integrity—tell the truth as you know it and be informed. At the same time, keep an open mind to hear and understand other people's truths.

To be a professional, dress the part, Clara advises—something that she has always held to be necessary. "If you want to impress somebody, you dress like you are going uptown, and you're going to buy the whole town," she says. "People respond to your appearance—if you look like you don't know what you're doing, people will believe that. When you are out and about as a leader, you have to look professional."

Staying active is essential in life because if you don't, Clara feels, you're letting your mind go. The same with clutter in one's life—it is vital to turn off the noise if you can manage it.

Keep your language clean because profanity doesn't accomplish much at all. Clara says, "I don't like cursing and swearing."

All in all, Clara says it's important to manage our time better and look at things positively. Look at the big picture, rethink your standards, and don't be afraid to forgive people.

"Don't try to control what is uncontrollable. Take time for fun, and keep your sense of honor," she advises. "Focus on the positive; look at the upside."

Clara Norgaard—Interview Insights

- Finding out who you are within yourself is not an easy task, but you can then find happiness, contentment, and success in your work and life once you know who you are.
- The key is to identify the stresses, understand what contributes to the stress, and take conscious, positive action to eliminate the stress.
- If possible, it is often best to avoid situations or people that create stress in our lives. If these situations cannot be avoided, it is important that we alter the situation, adapt to the situation, or accept that the situation exists.
- You must learn how to say no—avoid people that stress you out, take control of the environment, and avoid subjects you know will upset you.
- Express your feelings. Don't bottle things up inside. Be willing to compromise but be assertive.

Chapter 11

CHANGES YOU CAN MAKE NOW: KNOW AND LISTEN, TEST, TRUST, AND DELEGATE

"A good leader leads the people from above them—a great leader leads the people from within them."
—M. D. Arnold

"Don't follow the crowd, let the crowd follow you."
—Margaret Thatcher

"The growth and development of people is the highest calling of leadership."
—Henry S. Firestone

The Bible tells us that Joshua was told to be brave and courageous. I think this is a valuable skill to embrace because, as leaders, we are often called on to be brave and courageous.

It takes courage to make significant changes in your life, your personality, and your leadership style, but once you brave the change, these changes can be made in a relatively short time. By making these changes, we can move from struggling over to a state where we are working towards everyone being happy and productive—in small, manageable steps.

In this chapter, I'm excited to share some changes that you can make immediately in your workplace or whatever area you're contributing to help streamline each day.

Let's start with a big one: knowing and listening to your employees.

Know and Listen to Your Employees

Have you ever been in the company of someone who just doesn't listen to you? It can be very frustrating.

Have you ever been with a person who listened intently and made you feel like you are the only person in the world? Someone who validates you right away and who ensures that you know you have been heard? That sure is an interesting position, isn't it?

Now think about a person who doesn't listen, a person who is formulating a response right away. This person probably doesn't understand your point or totally misses it. Quite a different position to be in, isn't it? If you have been in the military or law enforcement, you have probably experienced this more than once.

I think we can all say that our listening skills could be improved. We've all seen suggestions such as, "You should listen twice as much as you speak because we have two ears and one mouth," haven't we? In the command-and-control structure, this skill seems to follow a slightly different path, more along the lines of, "Do as I say but not as I do."

I admit that I can struggle with this skill just as most of us do. I always seem to be preparing the response in the back of my head while trying to listen to the conversation and giving my total attention to the person I am trying to listen to.

So, how do you listen intently and actively?

Learning about and listening to your team, listening to whomever is in your presence—is necessary. Making your employees feel important and telling them you appreciate them goes a long way. Asking for clarification if necessary and validating their position gives that person ease.

If someone works for you, how they function, what they think about, how they work, their birthday, their spouse's name if they have one, their kids, and their interests are all basics that you need to know. If you develop a proper relationship with your employees, they will respect you and want a good relationship.

When you listen to what employees from the trenches have to say about being more efficient, they will usually be right on the money. Try to avoid a style that fights against change—if your attitude is, "We've always done it this way," and you feel that if it's worked before, it will work now, then you should rethink your plans and goals. That attitude is one that I heard many times in my law enforcement career, but the truth is that if an idea brought forward by your employees is legal, moral, and ethical, maybe it's worth considering a try.

During the 2010 Winter Olympics in Whistler, British Columbia, I managed a shift of 40 police officers. The interesting thing about this team was that they were from different police forces from all across Canada, making the job far more unique.

If you're not familiar with Whistler, it is a small community with a world-class ski hill, about an hour or so drive north of Vancouver. With the influx of people working at the 2010 Olympics and limited space during this time, space for an office was limited. Our office was a welding shop—not the most pleasant place. This was a negative starter for many of the members who were on the team there.

To make matters worse, a situation arose over some bottled water that showed up at the office that, believe it or not, was not from the proper sponsor—and because of that, could not be used. It was a huge headache.

The typical whining and complaining began. In a very command-and-control way, I was instructed to tell all my team members that this water could not be used. Instead of making a command-and-control instruction like the one I had been given, I decided to meet with everyone. Through discussion and listening well, we came to a workable solution. I brought this decision forward to the powers that be and, with some convincing, was able to get a workaround that was agreeable to everyone.

The most important lesson here was that I listened to the team first, respected their input, took it forward to the powers that be, and came back with the decision the team wanted. Not only that, they were all glad that I went to bat for them—this, too, was a total win.

Let me continue with a pair of other examples from my career, one where I wasn't listening; the other when I listened intently.

One of my employees presented his work to me, and I reviewed it. The work was not up to the standard necessary, and I commented on the review document that the work was deficient and needed further input. I also said in my note that I would be happy to give advice to help him move forward.

It turned out that the word "deficient" was not a word that was a good one in his vocabulary list, and, to be truthful, he had a meltdown. I couldn't understand what he was so upset about, and when he was responding to me, he was not at all polite or respectful.

I confess that things didn't end well.

If I had listened well, I might have understood that a previous supervisor had used the word "deficient" about him personally, and it was a very sore spot for him. At that point, I had no way to know, but I also wasn't listening. Later on, I managed to get things standing up straight again, but there is no doubt that our relationship was bruised and always needed to be treated respectfully.

On another occasion, a female employee came to me in tears. It was one of those very busy days that all offices experience, and I was stretched. I asked her if she would come into my office and she agreed.

She began to tell me about the incident. I told myself to listen intently and show her I was listening. I provided good feedback by asking if I understood correctly, and I did it in a nonjudgmental manner. Doing these small things well helped me understand the problem, and I could avert a potential crisis.

Normally on a busy day like that, I may not have listened as I should have, and this would have been a terrible mistake.

Listening well is probably one of the greatest tools in your box.

- How do we learn to listen well?
- Listen to learn, not to be polite. Ask questions when you need clarification.
- Quiet your agenda. Seek first to understand and then to be understood.
- Ask lots of questions; this validates the person you are with and brings clarity.
- Pay attention to your talk-listen ratio. As we said before, you have two ears and one mouth; listen twice as much as you talk.
- Repeat back what you heard. There seems to be more misunderstanding than understanding for some reason.
- Wait until the other party is finished talking before you respond. Even a moment of silence is okay.

Personality Tests

I find it interesting that we are all so different, and we all have so many unique gifts. We come from so many different backgrounds and cultures. This can be such a blessing, and yet it can be such a curse too, if not managed correctly. Sometimes personality differences are perceived as having a hidden agenda or being difficult. Often it is neither of these, but merely a misunderstanding.

Here is a case in point.

Late in my career, I had a new employee come to work for me. She was already in her late 40s, had two adult sons, and came with a wealth of work and life experience. She had worked in multiple agencies, and she and her husband ran a very successful construction business.

It had been her dream to be a police officer all her life, and at that time, with relaxed and more sensible recruiting standards, she was able to join—when she had applied previously, she hadn't met the physical markers in place at the time.

The first few weeks went fine, but then she started to exert her ideas and be verbal. My initial reaction was that she needed to keep her mouth shut and listen, but I could see that it would not happen. To deal with this, I needed to engage her with the proper parameters.

So, I gave her a personality test and interviewed her. I learned many things that I would not have known if I had not taken that step.

Her vast job experience gave her fantastic insight. She was a motivator, loved people, and wanted to do the job to the best of her ability. The biggest nugget I learned was that she was from an Italian background. Often, people from the Italian culture tend to be vocal and assertive, which was very different from my reserved British and Dutch background.

Knowing about her background became an essential piece of being a quality leader for her. She wanted me to listen to her first while she presented her ideas with gusto and flamboyance, and then when she asked my opinion, she was ready to listen and take advice.

I began to like working with her. Her reports were always very well prepared, and they were always timely. Crooks trying to get anything past her had a new lesson to learn too!

Give your team members a personality test and an interview if possible, so you know their skills, their background and family history, and how they fit into your team. This will help with delegation, improve your relationship, and build trust. If I had not given the lady above a personality test, we would likely have had quite a big mess. Had I followed my first instinct, which was to tell her to shut up and stay in her lane, it would have been a complete disaster.

You will be amazed at how this simple step can help you decide who gets a job because they are the most skilled, not because they are the most senior. Everyone has a skill and, as a leader, it's your job to find this out.

I took this step with all my new employees. Typically, your unit or company budget should cover this expense, and you should fight for it if you can—it's hard to communicate to you the value that it can bring to your knowledge levels and your team.

There are many great tests out there. Pick the one you like and find helpful and use it every time.

Delegation and Trust

When you want to stay calm at a stressful job or any situation, even your home, you will want to keep this section in mind—because it's huge.

Most managers and leaders don't know how to or don't want to delegate. Their mindset (Remember mindset? We talked about it earlier in the book, and here it is again!) is that no one can do it as well or as efficiently as they can.

This is terrible thinking.

When the workload is high, the stress meter is on bust, and you need help to get it all done, delegation is the key. You need to learn to delegate and trust the outcome.

Delegating successfully has many moving parts. Ask yourself: who can do this job best because they have the best skills? This knowledge is an area you need to work on, and in the process, you may get to know your employees or volunteers and what great people they are. They will appreciate it too, because you trust them, and they will be inspired to suggest better ways of doing the job.

Once you delegate a job, trust the person with it and be happy and complimentary with the outcome. Tell the employee that they did a great job. It may not have been done in the way you would do it. Still, as long as the starting and finishing points are correct, the resulting work stays in its lane following policies and procedures, and the functional requirements are covered, then let it go; trust the employee with the outcome.

I had a rule that I communicated to everyone on my team. It was kind of my line in the sand. If the decision could endanger others, waste taxpayers' money, or could damage government property, I had to be consulted and be in on the decision. Beyond that, I wanted my people to be innovative, solve problems, and be empowered to make decisions.

Now, please take note: in all of that description, I didn't say not to review the work, but let the person do the work. By all means, check in on things; just don't get in the way if you can avoid it.

Offer up suggestions if it looks like your chosen person could benefit from them—but don't do the work yourself. Learn to disengage from the outcome, and let it happen as it should. When you trust people, and you let them share and own the work they are assigned, you will find that they will excel; it's that simple.

The very odd time that someone fails, it's perfectly fine to say you are disappointed, but don't start the blame acquisition game. It's possible that your instructions weren't clear enough, or there was something else not understood somewhere along the line. Give that individual another shot. Most of the time, they just need a nudge or a suggestion because they are stuck; most people want to please a boss who will trust them and let them do their work. They feel valued when they contribute to the greater good of the organization and the team.

Recently when I was volunteering on a mission trip, I was in charge of the maintenance team. Most of the group were teenagers or young adults, with a sprinkling of middle and older adults.

Of course, my initial thoughts were to take the command-and-control route, bark out orders, and do as much as I could myself. For the first day or so, I ran around like a chicken with my head cut off. I'm sure from the outside view, I looked just plain stupid.

I finally had a little talk with myself, and soon I was delegating the workload, communicating clear instructions on how to do the job, and releasing the outcome. I used the same line in the sand from my law enforcement days: If the decision could endanger others, wasted money, or could damage property, I had to be consulted and be in on the decision. Beyond that, I wanted the team to be innovative, solve problems, and be empowered to make decisions.

I made a point of walking around and talking to everyone, checking in on how their projects were going. This built such trust and loyalty that I was floored, even at this level.

In this environment, the trust that this formed and the relationships that were forged were mind-boggling. Young people who would never approach me normally came to share their ideas and potentially better ways of doing their work.

I have to say, it was a great experience. Now, after the trip, these kids phone me and greet me on the street, and in fact, they want to sign on for the next mission trip on my team.

People, no matter their age, want to be respected, trusted, and valued. And, when you're delegating things to someone else, if you are a good listener, you may just learn something valuable—a better, more efficient way to do the tasks you have.

The skills of delegation and listening are some of the most important ones you can learn.

Too Much Paper!

In the early 1990s, I was part of an enforcement team on major highways in British Columbia, and one of our goals was accident reduction.

Resources were already stretched. Using those already stretched resources in the best possible way was the target. We regularly collected data to see where the high-incident locations were, intending to understand why crashes were happening there, and allowing us to deploy our resources to those locations where the most significant difference could be made.

The data we had, collected over five to seven years, was all on paper. To say there was paper everywhere was putting it mildly; the pile seemed to increase daily.

The person looking after this project wasn't making much headway. Sometimes we wondered if he was working. In all fairness, he was swamped. The data from that paper was analyzed. A pin was placed on a massive map of the area where we were working to show where the crashes were occurring. This was a great visual picture, but think of the logistics: imagine 50 crashes at the same location. How do you place a pin on a map in the same spot 50 times? I'm sure that you can understand that this was a total nightmare.

What did the management team say about this paper jam? "This is the way we have always done it." "Why would we change it?" "It's working."

As you can see, the command-and-control environment was in full effect.

One of the team members had an idea, though. He realized that if this data were all put into a database, it would be far easier to access and then reports could be generated at will, as well. He went to work on his own time and built this database. When he showed it to the powers that be, they (of course) were not believers, and the general view was that it would not work.

Remember, this was the early 1990s; computers were still relatively new, and many did not understand the benefits of using a computer for this type of work. One day a person on the executive leadership team recognized the potential that this database had. He took steps to get to know the member who developed it and was impressed with the outcomes being produced.

This leader was a visionary. He quickly assigned this project to that member, who saw that all the paper data was promptly and efficiently put into the database. As a result, the paper's stacks quickly disappeared, and the database became a useful assessment tool for the enforcement team.

Later, the database was adopted on a provincial basis in British Columbia before it evolved and grew even larger. It is now used on a Canada-wide basis.

This story's point is this. It's vital to know your employees and listen to their ideas, no matter how far down in rank they are. Then, delegate the work and trust that employee with the outcome.

To wrap up this chapter, let's look at a few steps that you can take to move forward in knowing your employees, listening better, and learning to delegate:

Decide to know and listen to your employees, your family, or your volunteers—have you learned about their skills and gifts? Were there things you were missing?

Were you able to give your employees a personality test, and what did you learn?

Delegation works for peace of mind and trust. Did you delegate work this week? What happened? Can you improve here?

Are you listening to your employees and giving them your undivided attention? Can you recall a time that happened this week?

Are you ready for the next steps?

Difficult People

By Robert J. Verbree

You're just causing problems and wasting my time
Was what I heard from an employee of mine.
We just couldn't agree to agree.
Always the need seemed to be about me.
This wasn't a new thing; this employee had come
From another department because he was a plumb.
But not of the right kind, no this one was rotten.
Of getting along, this one had forgotten.
It seems that no matter what anyone could suggest
Was just more ammunition for this one to undress.
One who loves a conflict, just must have their own way.
This has nothing to do with position or pay.
We see these persons away from work too.
At the shopping center, even the zoo.
They can't acquiesce or consider your view.
It's all about them and what they can do!
So, what is the solution to such irregular people?
Is what we see just a symptom of what's deeper?
I believe this is the case, for this is what is written.
For out of the overflow of the heart,
the mouth speaks and is smitten.
You best give wide berth to such people as this.
Stay out of this fog; stay out of this mist.
Or soon, like the bad apple in the barrel, you'll be,
rotten with negative thoughts, without glee.

When such a person is in your room,
Be careful with words, actions, and croon.
Grant them good day and shuffle along
To a place you're without their incredulous song.

Chapter 12

DIFFICULT PEOPLE, DIFFICULT EMPLOYEES, DIFFICULT BOSS

T oxicity in the workplace is widespread today. An astounding 76 percent of bosses are considered toxic by their employees, according to a groundbreaking Harvard University study done in 2015.

Exasperated employees and managers want to figure out how to address a toxic culture that is emerging at their companies. We also find this more and more in the home, as parents become stressed out and impatient with their children and teens.

The top four things that need to be in place for a healthy culture in the workplace and at home are communication, alignment, empowerment, and responsibility. Research shows that if any of these are absent, the atmosphere will be toxic.

When you work amongst selfish employees and managers who have zero self-awareness or any idea that they're coming across as self-centered, or employees who consistently act in selfish ways, a signal flare should go up pointing out that worsening toxic behavior lies ahead. One bad apple in the barrel soon spoils the entire barrel, as the saying goes.

When you recognize and understand that most companies, small businesses, and government departments put training at the very bottom of the budget list, this makes a lot of sense. Being trained to be an effective, contributing leader could bring so many positives if companies, families, small businesses, and other institutions understood the dividends that training would bring.

Training would remove so many of the unnecessary problems that come along. That's not to say things will be perfect. Problems will still happen, but with better tools available to leaders in the organization, those challenges are sure to vaporize.

I'm a firm believer that any time someone is promoted into a leadership position, that promotion should come with mandatory leadership training. The organization should make it compulsory for that staff member to complete their leadership training before getting the increase in pay tied to the job.

These days, training along these lines is easily delivered via the Internet—there's no excuse not to give it a try.

As a leader, the question that arises is how you should deal with situations where others are trying to derail your progress. Maybe they are jealous of you, fearful that you will take their job or undermine them, or they have just had no training—who knows?

Be assured that difficult people will come into your path and sometimes right into your lane. There is no shortage of critics. In 2005 the National Science Foundation published an article about research on human thoughts per day. They discovered that of the 12,000 to 60,000 thoughts everyone has in a day, up to 80 percent of them are negative, and 95 percent are exactly the same repetitive thought as yesterday. This follows through into the way most managers manage, as well: they have many negative thoughts.

Be assured that problems will always crop up when you are a leader with a plan. If you have a goal, and you are going somewhere, be ready for opposition. Knowing where you stand, being able to respond and not react, does take self-control.

You might ask, Bob, what is the difference between responding and reacting?

Here is a simple way to view this. You go to the doctor because you are ill. He says that he will give you some medicine and you should come back in two days. You return, and the doctor says, "Oh, you have reacted to the medicine—this is negative and needs readjustment." Or, he says, "You are responding nicely to the medicine—this is positive, and the way we need to proceed."

It can be very frustrating having to deal with people who are always complaining. Generally, the methods of dealing with complainers are these: you can ignore them, dump them, turn them over to someone else to deal with, or deal with them yourself.

If you choose to take this head-on and deal with it yourself, one technique I have often found successful is the pattern interrupt. This one takes practice but can be used effectively. While the complainer is in the midst of their complaining, interrupt them by saying, "Can I please ask you to pause for a moment and tell me what exactly it is that you want? Help me to understand what it is that you want."

Most of the time, they don't have a clue what they are complaining about—they are just emotionally spewing words spurred on by anger or frustration, probably motivated by a recent water cooler conversation with the other complainers on the team.

The next step is to validate them. Listen to what they're saying, acknowledge them, and say something along the lines of, "Aha; okay, continue." It helps if you synchronize your voice tone and overall body language with theirs while you're doing this. Let them get it out of their system. Typically, they're likely to dump all of this emotion in 90 seconds or less. Make sure you keep the person focused. If they drift off the point, bring them back to the center of their complaint.

Now motivate them by asking, "How would you feel if this problem was fixed?" Wait for an answer. Dig deep; don't accept an "I don't know." Continue in conversation and ask, "What else?" Repeat until they run out of things to say.

During this process, keep the person focused on one particular gripe. Then say, "Okay, so what would it take to fix it?" Encourage an answer. Listen, acknowledge, and say, "Aha." Ask, "On a scale of one to 10 with one being low and 10 being high, how motivated are you to fix it?" Listen, acknowledge, and say, "Aha."

Lastly, delegate. Ask, "What is the first step we should take?" or "How can we make sure this doesn't happen again?" or other similar starting points. Come to an agreement and take the first step.

Keep your advice focused, brief, and to the point, and don't ever say, "Things aren't so bad."

In my law enforcement career, I often dealt with critical and challenging people. Difficult people on your team or in your organization are the toughest ones to deal with, not the people from the outside. Many of these people are upper managers and middle managers. It sure seems like 80 percent of the people do all the work, and 20 percent do most of the whining and complaining.

This seems like it is pretty much universal, and these 20 percent of people take almost all your effort.

Here's an example, an event that happened early on at my new job site, right about the 28-year mark of my career.

I had just taken over my new department, which had been without a manager for 20 months. A senior employee on-site had taken over the manager's responsibility and kept things going while there was no supervisor. He did a great job considering the responsibility that he was given and his lack of rank compared to those who usually handled these particular positions.

This is a challenging role, being temporarily in charge until a new manager arrives, and then having to step back down to work with your peers. I didn't envy this employee at all.

A supervisor from another department seemed to take great pleasure in running down the people on my team with snide remarks and gestures. This had increased significantly while my team had been lacking a supervisor on site.

What was worse is that another very senior manager in the building chose to turn a blind eye to this problem. Although this supervisor was smiling and laughing when he spoke, there was no doubt in anyone's mind that his remarks were cutting, negative, and derogatory.

I asked him to stop this practice. He eased up—for a short time, at least, before the cutting remarks continued. Then I sent him an email and asked for a meeting; he didn't bother sending a response. At the end of the day in the dressing room, he unleashed his fury on me and widened the gap.

I did my best not to get upset; I stayed calm and listened. He went on and on and on about things that had absolutely no relevance, and he was bordering on being insane with anger because I had challenged him, and he was a rank higher than me.

To be clear, he had the ear of our boss because he was a golfer and a drinker—and I was neither. When I tried to keep him on track, he was so angry that the blood vessels in his neck were bursting, and his face was as red as a tomato. It was apparent that no one had ever challenged his ways.

At the end of his tirade, I respectfully told him that his negative remarks had nothing to do with teamwork and that he needed to stop. I also told him that he did not have a right to speak with such disrespect to me, and he needed to change it. It was time to set those boundaries.

He stormed out of the dressing room.

Wow, I remember thinking—I couldn't believe the negative spewing I had just observed. I went home thinking the war would continue. You can only imagine what kind of sleep I had that night—I was very concerned about what might happen the next day.

A day or so later, he asked to see me. When we talked, he apologized, said he was out of line, and he would change his comments.

I'm sure I didn't do everything right either. What I did, though, was stand my ground respectfully and set some boundaries, which in the end turned into a good result.

One of the more incredible benefits of this confrontation and its resolution was that my team knew I had tackled the problem directly—it had been a real irritant for them as well.

My team appreciated that I had stood up for them, which turned out to be a winning move—the team began to get on board with my vision and plans.

On the R-Y-G test, where do you think I scored with this resolution?

Take a few moments now, if you can, to think through this scenario. Do you see anything that I could have done differently?

Here is another example of dealing with difficult people from a different office setting. This is about Janice, a clerk for Max—remember him from our previous chapter on goals and vision, the transportation company professional?

Janice works in a hectic office with 10 other clerks, but her work area is on the opposite side of the building from the rest of the team, which is like working on her own. Janice is very pleasant, a very efficient worker, and always gets her tasks and much more accomplished in a workday. Whatever job Max gives her to do, she completes it promptly, and the result meets or far exceeds the standard expected.

If for some reason she doesn't wrap up her tasks during working hours, she stays until it is finished so that it meets deadlines. She is a great employee.

Janice is sometimes on her cell phone during work hours managing her kids, who are very important to her because she is a single mom. Sometimes she takes other personal calls as well.

Optically, this doesn't look very good. A complaint about this behavior was brought to Max by the clerks' office head. Her complaint stated that Janice must stop this behavior because some of the other ladies had observed this happening and were unhappy about it.

At the time, Max understood that other managers in the building did not like his plan to move forward; they viewed him as disruptive. To him, it was apparent that they were giving support to this complaint. Max believed that the other clerks were jealous of Janice's position away from the office head's overseeing eyes, who was a bit of a nitpicker. No one cared for her caustic management style either because it was entirely command-and-control.

Max, though, had expected something like this to come up. He requested a meeting with the clerks' head, as well as several of the senior managers. At the meeting, Max asked for the details of the incidents to be sure he understood the situation. He remained polite and receptive.

When his turn to speak came, Max pointed out that the clerks who worked on the opposite side of the office could frequently be seen wasting time in the lunchroom gossiping and finding all kinds of excuses not to work. Others were going outside hourly for a cigarette. Janice did not get involved in either of these behaviors.

Max then asked why he would cause friction about this when Janice was performing over and above expectations. Janice also had every right to launch a countercomplaint, which would probably cause an all-out war.

Max continued and said that if he needed to speak to Janice about this behavior in the interest of fairness, then the office head needed to talk to all the other ladies in the office about wasting time and going outside for smoke breaks. Max left the meeting, agreeing to speak to Janice—which he did. Of course, Janice's response was that she wanted a change from the other side of the office as well.

This is another one of those impossible situations where wisdom, self-control, and humility must be fully in place.

Ultimately the complaint was rescinded because they knew it was a nonstarter. Being respectful and standing his ground were the pieces of leadership skill that got Max around this barrier.

In this example, like the first one, we see unnecessary conflict from difficult people. This is going to happen if you are a leader in the digital age.

As I mentioned at the beginning of the chapter—and this is an excellent point to be reminded of since it comes up frequently—leaders face these challenges regularly, and never are they the same. Each and every situation has its particulars; however, learning the techniques in this chapter will help you make great strides forward in your leadership role. There are many great books written about this particular part of leading. I would encourage you to read further and master these skills.

Top Tips for Handling Difficult People

There are ideas everywhere offering ways to handle difficult people. I've collected a number of them here for you to consider:

- Listen: This is the best place to start when it comes to unreasonable people. Unless the person you're in conflict with understands that they're being heard, nothing will change. Everyone wants to be heard. Focus closely on what the other person is saying, and don't plan ahead for your next response.

- Stay calm: Don't get wound up in the conflict and recognize that you may face high emotion in some cases. Do your best to relax. Keep your breathing slow and regular, and if you feel the emotions building, take some deep breaths to calm down.

- Reserve judgment: None of us knows what another person might be going through, and we need to keep that in mind. It's possible they're feeling vulnerability or fear, and that's coming through in their actions.

- Show respect: Accept the other person's complaints and concerns with dignity—and allow them dignity as well. Don't show contempt, even if they're giving you a hard time—that is not a proactive approach.

- The hidden need: In being difficult, often people are trying to achieve, gain, or avoid something. Try to identify that for greater insight into their mindset.

- Look around for support: If you're dealing with something like an irate customer on the job, look around the area for colleagues who could help out.

- Don't demand compliance: If you tell someone who's upset to be quiet and calm down, they will probably get even angrier. Try asking them what the problem is, what's got them upset, and let

them blow off the steam. Don't feed them lines like, "I understand," but instead, "Tell me more, so I can understand better."

- Don't smile: Sounds counterintuitive, right? Well, if you smile
at someone who's really angry, they may think you're mocking
them. Good idea to avoid honor, as well—sometimes it can ease
a charged mood, but in other cases, it may backfire.

- Avoid acting defensively: It's natural to want to defend yourself when someone is in your face saying nasty things or offering up untruths, but when you're faced with a person in that
state, offering up a defense is not going to help. This situation,
remember, is not about you—try not to take it personally.

- Don't respond with anger: Again, if someone's spouting off in
anger, you're likely to want to return fire—but avoid this. Rais-
ing your voice, pointing your finger, and being disrespectful are
just ways to throw gas on the fire. Speak calmly, in a low, even,
monotone voice.

- Don't talk over them: Let the difficult person speak, and when
they take a breath, respond in the gap.

- Don't argue: It's never a good idea to try to convince a difficult
person of anything in the heat of the moment.

- Keep your distance: We often feel the urge to put our hand on
an angry person's arm or shoulder to try to calm them down.
Bad idea. In some contexts, this works, but upset people may
misinterpret it.

- Say, "I'm sorry": This simple phrase, or something like, "I'm
going to try and fix this," can help defuse touchy situations.

- Set limits: Venting is acceptable in some cases, but if the vent
turns to personal attacks, be assertive and tell the person, "Please
don't talk to me like that."

- Trust your instincts: If a situation seems to be going the wrong way, be ready to bail out and stay safe. Find a way to exit the situation if you need to.

- Situations change: Be flexible and be ready. While these techniques have often proven effective in de-escalating challenging situations, people differ significantly, and you never know how someone might react.

- Debrief: Once the situation's been cleared up, talk to somebody about it.

- Deal with your stress: You've had a hard day dealing with a difficult situation, and your natural reactions have been pushed back. Let that adrenaline go. Exercise, or walk the dog—do something different to break out of those emotions.

- Congratulate yourself: It's not easy to handle uncomfortable situations, and it takes a lot of work not to return the favor and act like a jerk when someone is doing it to you. Don't forget to congratulate yourself—you earned it.

A Stop at the Coffee Shop

Here is a scenario for you all to think about. This one happened at the coffee shop that my wife and I owned and operated.

Our company was very fair to our employees. We paid them above the industry standards, supplied complimentary food and drink when they were working, and provided a discount when they came in on their own time. We did our very best to treat all our employees with respect. Like any business in the service industry, without clients, you don't have a business. Top service is paramount, and it keeps people coming back.

One day, we arranged to come in for the day a little later than usual.

As we came in through the front door, we were greeted by a lineup of customers waiting to be served.

At first glance, we were pretty pleased by this situation because it meant that we were busy. However, when we got further into the store, we found that one of our employees was working very hard—and the other was on her cell phone, totally zoned out. Previously, there had been a meeting about staff using their phones during work hours, and we had all agreed that it would not be allowed.

When we mentioned that rule and said that she needed to get to work, she was visibly angry. In fact, for a day or so afterwards, she was challenging. When we asked her what was going on and tried to understand, she let us know she was having some personal problems and needed to be on the phone at that time.

There was more to the story than this, but what was very obvious was that we had a problem and one that needed to be dealt with sooner than later.

Now, let's turn our problem into your problem and use this as a learning experience. If you were in our shoes in this situation, using the steps listed above in this chapter—and through the book so far—make a plan to deal with this challenging situation. Keep the R-Y-G formula in mind as you do.

I'll include our solution in the next chapter—you can compare your answer to ours.

A Difficult Boss

If you have worked in any industry for a long time, you have probably worked for a boss who is autocratic, unreasonable, or bordering on lunacy. Wherever these traits come from—low self-esteem, lack of training, or wherever—this makes even the best job a grind.

One survey completed by the Gallup organization found that as high as 70 percent of North American employees feel that their boss is difficult or impossible, and they become actively disengaged. These characteristics seem to come out strongly in military-style organizations, but this is not exclusive.

Some bosses just seem heartless, and there appears to be no choice but to endure them until they self-destruct, get moved, or retire. They seem effective, somehow, and can slip past the magnifying glass of accountability.

These kinds of bosses develop a problematic mindset: they think they are omnipotent, possessing unlimited power and the ability to do anything they please. Some people wind up being promoted through the Peter Principle—they are promoted to the next level of incompetence. These types tend to be total autocrats who are on the verge of lunacy and self-aggrandizement.

Needless to say, these types of bosses should not be tolerated.

As a leader, you need to protect your people from them if at all possible. These types of bosses are dangerous—they can endanger every person in their organization and cause problems in every situation because they lose all perspective.

Many of the same factors in command-and-control organizations, where difficult bosses are often found, exist in other organizations. I have a friend in the real estate world who has told me about a colleague. This person is an excellent real estate salesman but an ugly boss because he thinks his title will carry him wherever he sets his sail. He now has the deluded idea that he is better than everyone else because he has moved up the ladder of success. Everyone admits that he is a good salesperson—but he is a horrible boss, as his lack of training and self-education show.

Leadership Failures

Let's look at this list of 10 major failures in leadership—many of them are certainly drivers in what causes people to be difficult, as well. See if you can pinpoint these in your leadership style, and if so, think hard about how best to remove them from your approach.

- The inability to organize details: A successful leader must be the master of all details connected with the position. This means that the skill of delegation must be learned and acquired.

- Unwillingness to render humble service: Truly great leaders are willing when necessary to perform any labor that they would ask others to complete. Lead by example.

- The expectation of pay for what they know instead of what they do with what they know: The world does not pay people for what they know; it pays them for what they do or how they influence others to do it.

- Fear of competition from followers: Able leaders train understudies how to do the job and help them excel. A leader who fears that one of his followers will take his position will most likely realize that fear. Said another way, what you think about expands.

- Lack of imagination: Without imagination, leaders cannot meet emergencies and create plans so the team knows where they are going.

- Selfishness: Leaders who claim all the honor for themselves will be met with resentment. Great leaders do not claim any of the honors.

- Lack of moderation or restraint: The team will not respect an intemperate leader. Lack of moderation or restraint destroys endurance and vitality.

- Disloyalty: Leaders who are not loyal to those below and above them cannot maintain their leadership.
- The emphasis of the authority of leadership: Great leaders lead by encouraging the team, not by instilling fear.
- The emphasis of title: Great leaders do not require a title to gain the respect of their team.

During my tenure in the law enforcement world, I worked for some great bosses, but some terrible ones as well. One horrible boss came at the end of my career.

I had known and worked with this person earlier in my career, and I knew what he was capable of. His one outstanding characteristic was that he treated everyone the same...very badly.

He was overbearing, did not listen, loved to demean, was a professional micromanager, and he could be just downright rude. When he took a senior management office, I knew what I would be facing. He was always all about himself and seemed to take great pride in belittling everyone on his team and telling them how great he was. His understanding of the operations was poor at best, and his management style was to pick on one small item and make a mountain out of it. It was just nuts!

When he did arrive, I had been managing my unit very effectively for four years. My team was happy. We were within our budget parameters and our metrics were above average. Then the dark cloud came. Darkness fell over the entire management structure.

People under his management, who had previously been good to work with, all fell into the bottomless dark pit too. At the end of my career, his insanity was the very last thing I needed. He micromanaged me, belittled me, dressed me down in front of my team, and on and on. After he was done with me, he sent his assistant to carry on with his caustic, cancerous, negative management style.

Shielding your team from this tyranny is painful and requires a lot of moral courage. I felt that failing to act and protect my team was cowardice.

To be completely honest, I didn't do a great job with it. In retrospect, I guess I was burned out. Things like this are the most challenging leadership situations to deal with, and I confess, it took years off my life.

Another boss I worked for earlier in my career was just autocratic. He had so many idiosyncrasies there wasn't enough paper to write about it here. In so many situations, his ideas were correct, but the way he communicated them to his team made everyone roll their eyes.

He couldn't get buy-in from others; the only thing that worked was his command-and-control system. He micromanaged everything, didn't trust his team, and didn't have much use for self-improvement or training. He seemed to want to keep everyone in a box so that they would not excel.

One day he asked me to write a memo to an outside agency. I went to my workstation, thought about the request for a while, and then remembered that he had recently sent out a similar memo.

When he left for the day, I went to our filing cabinet, retrieved his memo, and proceeded to write my memo using his outline. Then I submitted it and headed home.

The next day when I got in, the memo was in my in-basket with a note saying that this was the poorest memo he had ever read, and I was to fix it right away and resubmit it.

I went to his office and asked if I could talk about it. During that conversation, I told him that it was his memo with the corrections made to fit. His words, accompanied by an autocratic gaze, were, "It's not good enough; go and fix it and resubmit."

How do you respond to this?

I'm not sure! I just went and wrote another memo, resubmitted it, and never heard about it again. So yes, there are times when you need to know when to hold your cards, and there are times when you need to know it's time to fold up—simple as that.

Chapter 13

BE THE CHANGE: DISCIPLINE, COMMUNICATION, AND INTEGRITY

As we continue, this is an excellent time to talk about the fact that change does not happen automatically. By reading this book, we must realize that this is a starting point, and we will have to build on what we have learned so far. To quote Albert Einstein, "Only one who devotes himself to a cause with his whole strength and soul can be a true master." For this reason, mastery demands all of a person.

We often are told that it takes anywhere from six to 10 years to become great at something, depending on how often and how much you practice. Some estimate that it takes 10,000 hours to master something, but I believe that it varies from person to person, can depend on innate skills, and other factors.

Want to be great at leadership? It's possible to improve quickly and be great within a few years if you have the God-given talent and drive to do it—but most of us labor for a decade or more to master our craft and are still trying to get better. It takes practice, practice, and more practice.

With that in mind, let's go back to our scenario from the previous chapter when our employee was on her cell phone and the coffee shop was full of clients to be served. I hope you took the time to think that scenario through. Did you take a moment and write down a response or solution you feel would be the best approach? Practicing for these kinds of situations ahead of time and knowing what you are going to do will be a lifesaver for you in any incident.

I'm reminded of another police story that I'll share with you shortly, but first, let's consider our scenario and how we sorted it out.

We did not get angry with our employee. Instead, we asked for a private meeting and asked her to explain why she was on her phone when the store was so busy. As mentioned before, she told us that she was having problems at home and couldn't focus at that moment. We said we would help her where we could but emphasized that there would be no business without clients in our store—and her job would vanish with it.

As a result of the discussion, she apologized. We were happy with the outcome, as she was an excellent employee and we wanted to keep her.

If we had come to the meeting with both guns out, the outcome would have been much different.

This, I think, merits a Green on the R-Y-G scale, don't you think? Well, hear this: it came from practice, practice, and more practice.

Now, another police story. It involves discipline and communication, and several leadership points as well. It speaks to practice and to mastering these skills.

In the mid-1980s, I was working on the freeway, enforcing traffic laws. I had a great partner, and we got along very well. We frequently practiced scenarios and talked about what we would do when certain things happened, how we would manage them. One thing we spoke of often was that we would never give up our guns, ever. In the recent past, some police officers near us had given up their guns when challenged by a criminal, and the end result was not a good one.

Around this time, we were experiencing many high-speed car chases. Not only were these dangerous for the public, but many times the criminal was armed and ready to take action with his weapon too. We talked about what we would do and practiced our approach.

Wouldn't you know it—some weeks later, a call comes over the radio of a high-speed pursuit in progress coming towards us. Dispatch told us the driver was armed and dangerous. By this time, we both knew what we would do, and as the chase crossed over into our patrol area, we were ready for it. As we took over, we followed the suspect just as we had practiced and managed to force the driver to cross over a spike strip, deflating his right-front tire. The driver was soon running on the rim, and sparks were firing away from the metal.

What a sight it was, this car speeding along the freeway, with a light show blazing away from the right-front side. But it soon came to an end when the rim blew off and threw the car into the center median. As he came to a stop, my partner and I were out of our vehicles in an instant and ran to the suspect's car, sidearms drawn and ready—just like we had practiced.

When the driver saw us, he knew the gig was up. His hands were in the air, and he surrendered immediately.

Later, when we asked why he didn't try to fight, armed as he was, he told us flat out that he knew he'd be dead if he tried anything.

This event turned out well for us because we had practiced and mastered our skills—and the knowledge that we would never give up our guns, no matter what.

If you practice the leadership skills that are being taught in this book, the same result will come for you when the pressure is on. I can't say it enough: practice, practice, practice.

Discipline

Having the discipline to master any skill is very important. This is very true for leadership.

Discipline can be small things. It can start right at the beginning of your day, for example, by making your bed. This starts the day out right—you're tidying things up and removing clutter.

It may seem like a trivial thing, but here's an interesting point. If you take care of the small things, the big things seem to fall into place. I know that may seem curious, but here's the thing: it seems to work just fine.

Let's turn to one of the greats of self-improvement and motivation for a thought, shall we? Jim Rohn, talking about discipline, gave us this fantastic description to consider.

"If there is a magic word that stands out above all the rest, discipline is the one," Rohn said. "Discipline is the bridge between thought and accomplishment, the bridge between inspiration and value, and achievement. The bridge between necessity and productivity. Remember, all good things are upstream of us. The passing of time takes us drifting and drifting down the stream. This only brings us the negative, the disastrous, the disappointment, and the failure."

According to Rohn, failure isn't necessarily the collapse of everything all at once; it is, instead, a lengthy collection of small problems that catch up to you eventually. "Failing in life is failing to think today, failing to act today, failing to care, to strive, to climb, to learn, and to keep trying day by day."

Missing your goals might not seem like much during a single day. Rohn's example is that if your goal calls for you to write 10 letters in a day and you only manage three, then you're down seven. If you intend to make five calls and only make one, then you're down four. Trying to save 10 bucks today, and you don't, well, you're down 10 bucks, right?

It doesn't seem like that much of a deal until it starts to add up. Add those bad days up over a year, then add those years up over time—and you begin to see the problem that small failures, repeated regularly, can cause long term.

Success, though, is—as Rohn notes—the same process, just reversed. If you intend to write five letters and you write eight, then you are ahead three; make 15 calls instead of 10—and you're ahead of the game. Save $15 in a day instead of $10, and you're making money.

Be disciplined with yourself. Meet your goals and avoid those failures, and you will succeed in the long term.

Profound thought, isn't it?

Let's consider the definition of discipline. Dictionaries break it down as control gained by enforcing obedience or order; orderly or prescribed conduct or patterns of behavior; and—to me, the important one—self-control.

Here are some key points to consider when you're training yourself on discipline.

If you want anything to happen, it's totally up to you.

I like this quote by William Johnsen, "If it's to be, it's up to me." So many of the things in our lives require discipline. Think of this. If you move to a new town, just sitting at home and hoping you will make new friends won't work. It would be best to discipline yourself to get involved in the community, a group, or a gym. It is not just going to happen, especially if you're just sitting at home complaining!

If you want to write a book, just thinking about it won't work either—you need to take action and be disciplined. Write 200 to 300 words a day—religiously—to succeed.

Six Powerful Ways to Build Unbreakable Self-Discipline

- No matter what your goals are in life, there is one great law that you need to obey to be successful, and it is not procrastination. It goes like this. No one else will do the things you should be doing yourself or climb the ladder of success for you. No one else is responsible for your health, your wealth, your happiness, or your success. Only you can choose how you spend your time every day, every week, and every month. Having discipline or disciplining yourself will make it or break it. If you want a better life, you need to make better decisions and learn about discipline. You can blame other people for your lack of results or happiness all day long—or all life long, if you want to, but that doesn't change anything. Only you can change your life by changing the choices you make.

- Success does have enemies. The biggest enemy to success is the tendency always to take the path of least resistance. Remember the saying: some obstacles can become your best attribute. We must discipline ourselves to continue. Many go through life like a ship without a crew, with no destination in mind. It's like shooting arrows randomly into the air; you have no target to hit. If you choose leisure, what is fun and easy over what is necessary, you will never reach the levels of success and happiness you can achieve in your life. That's because every great victory requires great sacrifice. If success were easy, everybody would be successful. To achieve any goal you have in mind, you need three things: a clear vision for what it is you want; a plan to get to the target; and massive, consistent action repeated over time! The first two parts are the easy part of the equation. Most people struggle with the last part, the hard work and discipline to keep going. There is nothing that you can't achieve with hard work, so you must build the habit of choosing what is hard and necessary over what is fun and easy to do. Doing this is probably the surest way to succeed in life.

- Success is a long-term game. Abraham Lincoln once said, "The best way to predict the future is to create it." Have you ever thought about where you will be in 10 years from this moment? It's a great question to ask yourself because it allows you to focus on what needs to happen. What actions are you taking to make your goals a reality? How many books are you reading to grow as a person, how many online courses are you taking, and how many new things are you learning? Which people are you associating with? Are you disciplining yourself and putting in the effort necessary to achieve your goals today? Some people think that their lives will suddenly change through some magical event in the future, but that is not the case. We see this in people buying lottery tickets with money they can't afford, hoping they will hit the jackpot. Those odds are very, very low, of course, but they still put their faith into it. Your life changes only to the extent that you change. If you are not happy with your current circumstances—change them! Take action now. Nothing will ever change if you don't change what you do daily. As Aristotle noted over two millennia ago, "We are what we repeatedly do. Excellence, then, is not an act, but a habit."

• Walls, barriers, and obstacles are a part of success. Recently I was fixing a car I had bought and encountered a problem with the wiring that I just couldn't figure out. I spent hours looking over it and trying many different things to fix the problem. I just couldn't understand why everything could be so difficult, and to be honest, I was very frustrated. Finally, I succeeded, and the reality was, in the process of finding that success, I learned much more than if it had gone smoothly. I learned or honed skills I could use later on. Life seems to do that sometimes, doesn't it? It is often said that nothing worth having comes easy. You have to make sacrifices in the form of time, effort, pain, and hard work if you want to succeed. There will be setbacks, and any time you get close to finally succeeding, be assured there will be more adversity to test your armor, to see just how bad you want it. Only after passing one more test, and then another, will you be able to succeed. The great tragedy of life is that most people give up right before achieving success. An excellent read for this tip is the book *Three Feet from Gold* by Sharon Lechter and Greg Reid. The people who are the focus of this story were so close and gave up too early—just one more little push and success would have been theirs. Way too many people give up without finding the stuff to carry on to their end goal. For myself, I am encouraged very often by the words of motivational speaker Les Brown, "It's not over until I win!"

- Write and recite your goals every day. To grow and maximize your self-discipline every day, you must keep your goals in mind. Some call this knowing what your "why" is. Nietzsche once said, "He who has a 'why' to live for can bear almost any 'how.' " I believe this to be true. Sometimes, when life is happening, we can forget what our why is, what our target is. To this point, here is my solution. I write a thankfulness journal every day, and I also write out my intentions and goals for the day. Yep—every day. Some days I don't feel like it, but, as they say, I just do it. I am not just saying this, reader. I can show you notebooks full of my writings. I also make a point of reciting my goals throughout the day. This embeds them in my mind and helps me keep my "why" in focus. Only when you are focused on your goals and your vision for your life are you truly able to make decisions that contribute to those goals.

- Make a firm decision in advance that you will never give up. Again, I want to mention Les Brown's key phrase above—it is never over until you win, as long as you push for it. It's hard to stay strong in the face of adversity. To make sure that you stay strong in the face of adversity, make sure to resolve in advance how you will respond. As I mentioned earlier, practice is important—which I illustrated with how my partner and I handled that suspect. Call what we did playing cops and robbers if you want, because that's kind of what we did. But the truth is, the time came more than once when we needed to respond in the face of adversity, and we already knew what our response would be. You need to have a plan for what to do when everything goes south, or else it is too easy just to give up. When writing your goals, commit to making them come true, no matter how hard it may be. Determine how you will respond to failures and setbacks so you can bounce back stronger and better than ever before. If you commit and never break it, you will succeed at anything you set your mind to.

Communication

Let's discuss communication. This is a big part of leadership because if you want to be able to work well with your employees, boss, and family—and to be able to get along with anyone—you need to be a good communicator.

A leader cannot work in isolation. Leadership begins with a vision. The leader's task is to communicate the vision, the mission, and the goals to his people with respect and humility. To make that work, a leader must be first and foremost a communicator. The ability to communicate through speech, writing, and electronic means is a leader's most valuable asset.

In every professional environment, it is essential to communicate effectively with your peers. This is particularly true during meetings, in which people expect to discuss a subject, reach conclusions, and make related decisions quickly.

I want to present seven rules for effective communication for you to review. If we leaders followed these simple rules, communication would be more effective!

As an interesting aside, these seven rules aren't new; in fact, they were written more than 2,000 years ago—in a Jewish book of ethics called *Pirkei Avot*. These rules apply just as well today as they did when they were first discussed way back then…isn't it a good idea to look to our past as a way of shaping our future?

Respect Experience and Seniority

There is a significant difference between knowledge and experience. Sometimes it's hard to believe, but most people reach senior positions through real competence and accomplishments. Thus, you should always listen carefully to what the veterans have to say, even if it appears wrong. Most probably, they can see something that you can't, so if you disagree with their opinions, first ask them to justify their point.

How can you be respectful of experience and seniority?

Don't Interrupt the Speaker

If you are participating in a meeting, you should be very interested in understanding what the other participants have to say. But by interrupting others, you are not allowing them to communicate their opinion clearly. This is, first of all, a sign of disrespect that may cause bad feelings. But interrupting others also gives them the right to interrupt you, creating a chain reaction with very negative consequences.

What can you do for yourself so you do not interrupt the speaker?

Think Before You Answer

Of course we must think if we are unsure about the answer, but we must also think even if we could answer immediately. When participating in a meeting, we are not only interested in expressing our views, but we also must also explain and justify our opinions. When we know that someone may disagree with us in advance, we need to think about presenting our ideas clearly and solidly.

How can you help yourself to think before you answer?

Focus on the Subject

For meetings to be effective, we must focus on the topic being discussed. There is a limited amount of time available to conclude, and we don't want to waste this time with similar issues. If other important topics need to be discussed, they should deserve their own meeting. When answering someone, always address the question directly, and never ask questions that are not related to the discussion.

How can you train yourself to focus on the subject?

Organize Your Presentation

When answering a question, you should define your priorities. Say the most important things first and add more comments only if they are necessary. If you were asked several questions, answer them in the same order they were asked, or explain plainly what your approach is. Ask for clarity if necessary. Also, answer each question separately. It will be much easier for the other participants to understand you if you present your thoughts clearly.

How can you help yourself organize your presentation?

Understand That You Don't Know Everything

If you are asked a question for which you don't have a good answer, it's perfectly natural to say that you simply don't know. Of course, you should know the answer to any question directly related to your tasks. But when the topics being discussed are related to the work being done by teams of people, you're not expected to know all the details.

How can you help yourself accept that you don't know everything?

Don't Argue the Facts

You should have your personal opinion about all the important issues being discussed. This is the contribution that the other participants expect you will bring to the meeting. You should know how to explain and justify your opinions. At the same time, you should also know how to stop debating when presented with new facts that contradict your view.

How can you help yourself so you don't argue with the facts?

Integrity

There is lots of talk today about integrity, but so many don't know what it means.

Merriam-Webster defines integrity in three different ways. First: firm adherence to a code of especially moral or artistic values. Consider this as "incorruptibility." Second: an unimpaired condition—think "soundness." Third: the quality or state of being complete or undivided—or "completeness."

So, is it doing what you say you will do, or what you say you will do when no one is looking—or a combination of both? Well…it's both.

Doing what you say you will do when you said you would do it, even if it hurts, would be close. It's about following through on what you say if things go wrong, as they sometimes will.

Not a person on this planet is perfect. If you are wrong—admit it. This goes without saying, in my mind, but many people make excuses and justify their actions. If you were wrong or out of line, accept responsibility and call it square.

The last part of the definition is complicated: doing what you say you will do even when no one is looking. No taking any liberties, no hidden agendas. Most people will slack off when the boss is not around.

But why not build a culture of doing it the right way every time, no matter what?

Apple, as an example, has built an entire business model on this one concept. When you buy their products, they work—and they stand behind the quality. How about a person who picks up a wallet with $1,000 inside and returns it to the owner all intact? Many of us who hear stories like that say, "Wow!" We're surprised when this happens. But… isn't that the way it should be—the way you want it to be? It's never anything to feel guilty about, just pure integrity.

Here's a good one from my career that fits well in a discussion of integrity. I once was called to a car accident in which the driver was heading home from a gambling weekend. He fell asleep at the wheel, swerved off the freeway, and hit the concrete rail at the roadside. His car flipped onto the roof, smashing all the glass out.

Sadly, the gambler had made his last bet. I was the first person to respond to the scene. It was unique for one reason: the man had been transporting quite a lot of money—and it was scattered all over the place. What a sight—it looked as if it had been raining money.

It would have been easy to pick some of that money up. Not a soul would have known. The accident had happened in a very rural area.

I don't think there is a person on the planet who wouldn't have had that thought. Instead, I knew that this was a serious situation. I called for other members on duty to come out and help pick the money up. We were cautious collecting and storing those funds, and every dollar was returned to the gambler's wife.

On another occasion, I was working in the office when a man came to the front counter. I could tell he was a street person and not well off.

He put a wallet on the counter and said he had found it while walking on the main street. There was $1,500 inside it. This man said everything was inside, and he had not touched anything.

Again, he could have kept the lot for himself, and no one would have been wiser.

When I called the owner, he was—to say the very least—relieved. When I asked him how much cash had been inside when he lost it, he said $1,500. I was quite shocked—but at the same time, I was also reminded that this was precisely the way I would want to act, every time, even when nobody was looking.

Integrity—it's a massive piece of leadership, and frankly, it's kind of catching!

Accountability

Back to Jim Rohn for a moment. He famously said that we are the average of the five people we spend the most time with. That, as we established previously in this book, is true. If you hang out with negative people all the time, soon you will be negative too. If you hang out with successful people, most likely, you will be a success also. So, if you want to be accountable, hang out with accountable people. Right?

Many businesses, senior executives, leaders, and management teams want to talk about the topic that is always difficult to broach—accountability—but how do we make it work?

Most people don't understand what accountability is, why it's important, or where it starts. Yes, they understand accountability is necessary. The problem is, they don't know how to create a culture of accountability and just hope it will happen. I don't think that is the correct approach. I fully believe that accountability is a skill that has to be developed and exercised.

According to our friends at *Merriam-Webster*, accountability is the quality or state of being accountable, especially an obligation or willingness to accept responsibility or to account for one's actions.

With that in mind, let's talk about some things that will better help us understand and increase our accountability.

Accountability starts with you. This is a bold statement, but it's absolutely correct. It would be best if you modelled the behaviors that you want to see in your organization. If you want people to take ownership, then you have to be seen to take ownership. When you make commitments, you have to be seen to meet those commitments.

Another story from my policing career is applicable here. Some of the young guys on my team let it be known that I didn't have what it took to write the number of traffic tickets I required them to produce every day. Without saying anything, I got myself out on the road every day despite all the additional office work I had on top of the outside duties.

It meant I had to put in many more hours than the young guys, but I knew that the accountability this type of action would show was critical to my leadership of this team. At the end of the week, wouldn't you know it—I was the top ticket writer, hands down. This accountability was huge for me. Moving forward, my team understood I knew what was expected of them—and that I could keep up and exceed what they were doing.

As a leader, you are accountable. You're accountable for any failures, as well as any successes, that your organization may have. Accountability comes as part of the job description, so if you try to duck it, it will negatively impact you. If it is your problem, your failure, or your success, you need to own it. As the story above shows, your team will know it, either way.

Accountability is not a one-time, sometimes thing; it is front-page news all the time. Your team and your adversaries will always be looking. It's an all-the-time thing. Those people who don't want to be accountable, or don't want to be held accountable, are always looking for any opportunities to get out of it—or they just push the blame elsewhere. Remember: the blame game never ever works. It always backfires. Any slips or gaps in your accountability will give them the out they need and let them only be accountable when they see fit. You need to be seen as accountable at all times.

Accountability applies to everyone. When you are trying to hold people accountable, you cannot play favorites. You must be consistent across the board; you cannot let it slide with some people. Accountability has to be consistently applied to everyone, all the time.

If you choose to let one person ignore their accountability, it opens the door for others to be selectively accountable.

Got it? The message here is simple. Hold the accountability torch high and apply it evenly and consistently.

You cannot delegate accountability—period. Accountability has to be accepted so your whole team can feel accountable, so they want to take ownership. Make sure you have the entire process set up so that everyone can be successful. No one will take ownership and show accountability for something that they know, or believe, will fail.

If you want people to accept accountability, ask them if they have everything they need to be successful. A "yes" says they have taken a big step towards accepting accountability. A "no" suggests you need to make sure to provide whatever is missing because, without it, they will never accept accountability.

Here is a key insight for you: accountability is the difference between success and failure. When people don't see the need for accountability and don't feel ownership, disaster is near.

When things go south (and don't be naïve because they will), your team's dissenters will go into spectator mode and watch as things fail. If they thought it would fail from the outset, it's even worse because then they go into "told you so" mode—and that nearly always becomes a self-fulfilling prophecy.

When people take ownership, if things start to go wrong, they step into solution mode, and that is precisely where we want to be. Right away, they will begin to determine what is going wrong and try to fix it. Successful teams are full of people that go into solution mode. They are full of people who not only care but also take care. In my experience, accountability is the single biggest differentiator between successful and unsuccessful teams.

Be sure to keep in mind that you, as the leader, have to hold people accountable. You can't just tell people they're accountable. You need to set up review sessions; you have to check in and see how people are doing. Remember: what gets reviewed gets done. This lets the team know that they will be held accountable for the activities they are part of. It allows you to provide support if things start to go awry and offers you the opportunity to give praise and encouragement to move people further if things are going well.

Accountability is something that has to be worked at. There has to be a clear and consistent strategy on how it will be implemented and validated. It starts with you, and it has to apply at all times and to everyone. When you can do that, it will help you create a culture of accountability where the organization will start to hold itself and others accountable. Having that as an organizational goal—and making sure it happens—will have a massive impact on performance and results.

Chapter 14

GREAT LEADERSHIP IS ABOUT WISDOM, NOT INTELLIGENCE:

Self-Control and Humility

A s we get towards the tail end of this book, I hope you've been enjoying this journey as much as I have. It's quite a fantastic adventure, isn't it, getting to good leadership? But—we still have a few more things to learn, and in this chapter, learning is one of the things that we'll check out. Not bad, huh?

Sometimes people get deep into a project—like, say, developing leadership—and then, they run out of steam at the halfway point or near the end, and they don't complete the project. I hope that you stay motivated and keep pushing it forward.

I love stories, so…here's a story that's very relevant from author Zig Ziglar's book *Biscuits, Fleas, and Pump Handles*.[9] Zig was a very dynamic motivational speaker. I have been privileged to attend a number of his seminars, and he's always provided plenty of food for thought. In this case, it's a little story he called "Prime the Pump."

Zig tells the story about a pair of friends, Bernard and Jimmy, driving through rural Alabama on a hot August day when they got really thirsty. So they pulled off at an old abandoned farmhouse. One of the men headed for an old well there on the property and started pumping the pump. After a few minutes of pumping, he said to the other man, "Better get that old bucket over there and get some water out of the creek—we're gonna have to prime the pump." That means pouring some water into the top of the pump to get it to start working. After priming the pump and some more pumping, Bernard tells Jimmy that he doesn't think there's water down there. Jimmy assures him yes, there is water down there. Finally, Bernard gets disgusted with this whole process. He throws his hands up and tells Jimmy that there just isn't any water down that hole. "Don't stop pumping, Bernard, don't stop, because if you stop, all the water you pumped up the pipe is going to go all the way back down, and you're going to have to start all over." The question here really is, how much pumping are you going to do for a drink of cold water? The idea in the story continues…

"A lot of people stand in front of the stove of life, and they say, 'Now, stove, you give me some heat, then I'll put some wood in you,'" Zig says. "This is not the way that it works. You got to put something in before you can get anything out."

Think about an employee who goes to the boss and says, "Give me a raise, and then I'll start coming to work on time," or they say, "Make me the manager now—I know I haven't been here very long, and I don't deserve to be the manager, but I just function better when I'm in charge of things. You reward me now, and then I promise you

I'll learn what this business is all about later on. Reward me now, and I'll produce later."

Imagine the sight of a farmer standing in his fields in October, saying, "Lord, I know I didn't plant a thing this year, but if you give me a big crop, I'll plant more than anybody else next year."

Zig reminds us, telling this story, that things don't work that way—you have to put something in before you can expect to get anything out.

That is the truth of life. Anything worth doing is worth doing correctly and completely. We don't know how many kids have missed out on a college scholarship because they didn't study an average of 10 more minutes a day and how many people missed a promotion because they got discouraged and quit too soon. There's success to be had as long as you put something in, and then pump—and pump—and pump—and pump some more.

"I believe, with all of my heart, that if you pump long enough and hard enough and enthusiastically enough, that eventually, the reward is going to follow," Zig says. "Then, once that water starts to flow, all you gotta do is just keep a little easy, steady pressure on it, and you're going to get more water than you can possibly use."

Many people today seem to have the philosophy, "I'll give it a try, and if it works out, that will be good, and if it doesn't work out, that's okay too, I ain't gonna kill myself." That's a recipe for pumping forever, Zig assures, before anything actually happens.

"When you get going on something, grab that pump handle, and get with it—and then once the water starts to flow, all you gotta do is keep a little steady, easy pressure on it," Zig advises.

Now, the point of that story should be easy to spot, especially for leaders like you. Here's how I interpret it. When you are trying to go somewhere or improve your position, you need to give it lots of hard work and effort.

Learning to be a leader requires just those efforts. It will take you a lot of work and time to get better and become an effective, quality leader. I hope that you'll keep this in mind. Don't get discouraged now. Don't quit. Give it all you've got.

Wisdom and Intelligence

"Who is wise and understanding among you? Let them show it by their good life, by deeds done in humility that comes from wisdom." That sentence, from James 3:13,[10] is a great starting point for discussing wisdom. In Proverbs,[11] we also find words about wisdom: "The fear of the Lord is the beginning of wisdom, and the knowledge of the Holy One is understanding."

The first step in where wisdom starts from and how one becomes wise is understanding just what wisdom is and why we should be wise—and why wisdom and knowledge or intelligence are not necessarily the same in the grand scheme of things.

The dictionary definition of wisdom is "the ability to discern or judge what is true, right, or lasting." On the other hand, knowledge is "information gained through experience, reasoning, or acquaintance." Knowledge can exist without wisdom, but not the other way around. One can be knowledgeable without being wise. Knowledge is knowing how to use a gun; wisdom is knowing when to use it and when to keep it holstered.

Wisdom is very much an essential part of being a good leader. It is so interesting how all the leadership pieces are intertwined and how one piece needs the others to work.

There's a difference between knowledge, information, and wisdom.

Information can be gleaned from newspapers and magazines. You gain knowledge by reading good books and articles. But until you add the spiritual dimension, you're missing the wisdom—or what some people prefer to call common sense. That's the reason some leaders who are geniuses in one department drop the ball in so many other departments. Their common sense or wisdom is missing.

How do you find wisdom, though? Well, that's the big question, isn't it?

Ancient scripture tells us that one must listen and open the spirit wide to expand your discernment. You have to search for it like a miner searches for gold or like a pirate searches for hidden treasure. The result is that it will appear—but only if you keep at it.

I like the way Solomon, son of David, King of Israel, defines wisdom. We're told in Proverbs[12] that "the fear of the Lord is the beginning of wisdom, and knowledge of the Holy One is understanding. For through me your days will be many, and years will be added to your life. If you are wise, your wisdom will reward you; if you are a mocker, you alone will suffer."

To my eye, this says strongly that a spiritual aspect is in play here and that it's an important dimension that must be present for one to acquire true wisdom.

We often think of seniors as having more wisdom, but we also know that cognitive function can decline in our older years. Young people can retrieve information far more quickly than older adults. According to a study by Tilburg University, seniors show "greater sensitivity to fine-grained differences" in knowledge. Since they have more life experience, they can detect familiar "patterns" more readily than younger adults.

With all that in mind, we must ask, how do you develop wisdom? Well, here are some tips that I think may be helpful.

- Learn from your experiences. Don't show off what you already know—see what you can learn.
- What have you learned from your life experience?
- Be a student of your own life.
- What have you learned about yourself?
- Nurture self-awareness. Work on seeing yourself clearly, all the time.
- How have you nurtured self-awareness?
- Think about others first. How can you think of others' needs more?

Self-Control

Self-control is defined as the restraint exercised over one's impulses, emotions, or desires. It helps us change and regulate our responses to avoid undesirable behaviors, increase desirable ones, and achieve our long-term goals.

Without self-control, people find themselves having serious problems. Think about it; without self-control, how would that weight-training program go? Not very well, right? How about the dieting after Christmas or the pledge to give up your daily drive-through run to save some money? Regular exercise, healthy eating, getting things done on time, pushing away bad habits—without self-control, we'd all find ourselves in trouble.

Research suggests that self-control is a limited resource. Over time, when we practice and focus on maintaining that self-control, it becomes more robust—but in the short term, it can be limited. We must practice before we are required to use it before it is needed. When we focus on fighting off one urge, it can often be challenging to do it again later in the day.

We've all seen a lack of self-control in our life journeys, and most of the time, it is difficult to be around, and it is offensive. Like all the qualities of leadership, self-control must be carefully developed and nurtured. A life of discipline, making decisions ahead of time, gratitude for adversity, ruling your spirit, and controlling your thoughts takes a lot of work and practice—but it can be done.

The Story of Jackie Robinson

Jackie Robinson was born on January 31, 1919, and died on October 24, 1972. In his 53 years, he accomplished amazing feats for himself and all of humanity. Brooklyn Dodger fans who saw Jackie Robinson take the field in 1947 witnessed more than just a great ballplayer; they experienced history in the making.

Robinson broke the color line of professional baseball. He was the first African American to play on a major league baseball team.

Robinson was the perfect man for the job. He was multitalented in a variety of sports, but his most extraordinary talent, it could be said, was how he worked through and dealt with all of the abuse he faced.

Jackie Robinson's self-control appeared to be superhuman. Robinson had great courage, self-control, fierce determination, and believed in social action. Being the first African American to play on a major league team wasn't easy. Baseball fans booed and yelled ugly names. Players threw wild pitches and dug their spikes into him as he slid for home. Racists sent death threats.

With the strength of his convictions and his strength as a person, Robinson prevailed.

Through his quiet control, bravery, and commitment, Robinson gained the respect of fans and players. He became a symbol for Black opportunity.

At the end of that first season, he won the Rookie of the Year Award, and forty years later, the award was renamed in his honor.

Jackie Robinson's self-control was second to none and provides us with a stellar model to look up to.[13]

The Story of Bron Clifford

Bron Clifford has been described as a young fireball evangelist, a powerful young preacher who, in 1945 at the age of 25, started a career in the church alongside such eminent evangelical figures as Billy Graham and Chuck Templeton. He was a real up-and-comer in the church, and people were lining up for hours to hear him preach.

During one event at Baylor University where Clifford was scheduled to appear, someone cut the bell tower's ropes—they didn't want anything to interfere with his preaching. And, that day, for two and a half hours, the students were on the edge of their seats listening to Clifford's fiery presentation on "Christ and the Philosopher's Stone."

Bron Clifford was a tall, dashing, handsome figure who was sophisticated and intelligent. World leaders sought his counsel. He set more attendance records than any other clergyman. Hollywood directors called on him for starring roles. He seemed to have everything indeed.

And yet, less than a decade after that great debut on the world stage, Bron Clifford had lost everything—including his life. The reason? An addiction to alcohol that he didn't have the self-control to manage.

Clifford died from cirrhosis of the liver at the age of 35 in an Amarillo, Texas, hotel. It was a tragic end to a promising career. He left his wife and two children with Down syndrome penniless, and a group of pastors from Amarillo collected enough money to buy a cheap casket. Clifford's body was sent back to the East Coast, where he lays buried in a pauper's grave.

As we can see from this story, even those who are leaders in their own right can fall away from those heights, succumbing to pride, immorality, discouragement, love of wealth, or other vices.[14]

In sharing these stories, I want to illustrate something important: the differences between these two men. Many people cannot handle the status that comes with being a leader. When a leader can exercise self-control, you will find it is nearly impossible to knock them down.

On the other hand, lack of self-control is capable of destroying leadership. Self-control gives the leader the courage to stand alone and not be diverted from his vision by others' opinions and the crowd's subtle pressures. Self-control draws followers to the leader. People like to follow a leader who demonstrates self-control. Like all principles of being a leader, self-control must be carefully developed and nurtured.

Self-control is an essential skill that allows you to regulate behavior to achieve your long-term goals. People with great self-control tend to do better in school, have higher self-esteem, and better physical and mental health. While self-control is a limited resource, research also suggests that there are things that you can do to improve and strengthen your willpower over time.

Improving Self-Control

According to psychologists, there are many tips and techniques that we can use to strengthen our self-control. Let's look at a few.

Avoid temptation. It seems simple, right? Just try saying that when someone's offering you a big slice of pie when you're dieting. It's not easy to avoid temptation, but it's an effective method to use your available self-control to the best of your ability and lets you save it up for when it's really necessary.

What are some of the ways you can avoid temptation in your life?

Plan ahead. Think about how your resolve might be tested, and if that temptation comes along, how you will respond to avoid giving in. Research shows that planning improves your willpower and self-control, even in very challenging situations.

How can you plan in your life?

Practice using self-control. Yes, you may run short on self-control in the short term, but if you regularly practice the behaviors that require you to exert self-control, your willpower will increase over time. It's a lot like regular exercise. When you do a lot of bicep curls in a short time, your biceps will become exhausted—but they will grow every time you work out. Do this with your self-control as well.

How can you practice your self-control?

Focus on one goal at a time. If you set too many goals all at once, it's almost certain that you're not going to achieve them. You use your will-power in one area, and your self-control can be reduced in other areas. Be smart and pick one specific goal to focus on at any one time. When you have made the behaviors that help you achieve that goal into habits, you don't need to devote as much effort to maintain them—and you can use those resources for other purposes.

What self-control goal do you have in mind to change?

Humility

Among the many vital attributes that leaders need to develop if they wish to have a meaningful impact in their workplace, home, or elsewhere, one seems to be overlooked frequently: humility.

In part, this is likely because of common misconceptions about what humility is and what it means to be humble. The truth is, humility is one attribute that no leader should do without. False humility, which some leaders even work towards, is where the person is very proud of acting humbly, but in actuality, is arrogant and promoting self-aggrandizement.

Humility tends to be overlooked in the workplace because it is frequently misconstrued as a weakness. Truthfully, humility brings tensile strength to leadership. We have been led to believe that humble people are easily bulldozed by others and aren't willing to stick up for themselves.

Many define humility as having a low opinion of oneself. This is just incorrect!

So, how do you describe humility? I like this definition: humility gives tensile strength to leadership. That is undoubtedly a long way past a low opinion of oneself. Part of the greatness of humility is the ability to rise above your sensitivity of others' opinions concerning yourself—in other words, you are not easily offended.

Can you meet criticism with tranquility and pleasantness? If you can, this helps you to rise to your full potential as a leader.

I confess this is one tip that I have struggled with greatly. When my wife corrects me and looks out for my best interests, I am often motivated to retaliate at what I unconsciously perceive as her trying to control me. This seems to be a good starting point for me to work on my humility!

A humble person is free from pride or arrogance; he or she submits themselves to others and is helpful and courteous. A humble person does not consider himself self-sufficient, yet he knows his gifts, resources, and achievements. A humble person does not take offense or fight back.

Humility is also not cowardice either, because humility requires high courage. Humility makes you the leader willing to take a lower place than you deserve, or to keep quiet about your merits, to bear slights, insults, and false accusations for the sake of a higher purpose.

Humility today is a far cry from the true meaning of the word and how it should be applied in leadership. Humility isn't about being passive and weak. It's about showing respect and recognizing the truth in all situations, including in the workplace, home, or business.

In contrast to the idea of humility as weakness, *Merriam-Webster* defines the word as "freedom from pride or arrogance." It is listed as an antonym for words like "egoism," "conceit," and "superiority."

C. S. Lewis shared one of my favorite quotes on this subject: "Humility is not thinking less of yourself; it's thinking of yourself less." In other words, a humble professional sounds like the type of person that most of us would prefer to interact with daily. It is the type of person that can become a truly effective leader.

If you've already found success in the business world, it can be tempting to dismiss others' feedback or criticism. But this leads to stagnation and pride; not all criticism is indeed valid. Professionals who don't have much humility tend to dismiss all criticism, or worse, blame others for their own mistakes. Humble leaders must be willing to evaluate criticism to determine if it's valid or not. The best leaders are willing to admit when they are wrong and view mistakes as learning opportunities so that they can turn them into something positive—something transformative. If I could give them any attribute with a wave of a magic wand, it would be humility.

A study published in the *Journal of Management* highlighted just how far-reaching the effects of humility in leadership can be. The study concluded that humble leaders were far more likely to delegate and innovate. As a result, company performance and employee satisfaction improved, while turnover fell. In other words, humble leadership essentially empowers employees. They become more willing to speak their minds and offer suggestions because they know their leaders will listen.

This culture of humility results in high engagement and innovation—and if there's one lesson that has been consistent in the business world, it's that innovation is crucial if you want your success to be sustainable in the long run. Though the world often underrates humility, it's essential to be successful as a leader, not just at work, but also in life. Reject your notion to boast or lift yourself above anyone and decide to be at the service of others.

One day, in the later stages of my career, I was on a vacation day. My wife was working, all my children were grown and out on their own, and I wanted just to relax. I was unshaven in shorts and a ball hat, probably not recognizable as the police officer in charge of the area's traffic section.

I took myself off to the park. It was a nice, warm day in late spring, and I was sitting on a park bench just basking in the sun. Looking out over the lake, I could see the Canada geese loping around on the grass and hear their familiar honking. Fish were jumping for the mosquitoes in the lake. The tranquility was great. The lake was like a mirror.

After maybe a half-hour, a middle-aged man of some stature in the community came and sat on the bench near me. He started the conversation with typical greetings—"Hello, how are you?" and so forth. Soon, though, he was talking about a tragic motor vehicle incident that had occurred several days prior. As he continued with the details he had acquired, he became more and more animated about the fact that the police were useless and more interested in going for coffee than working.

His tirade continued, belittling the investigation and how poorly it was handled, and he asserted that the guy in charge—me—was a total idiot.

He had absolutely no idea who he was spewing all this verbiage to.

My first reaction was to retaliate and tell him where it was at because mostly his words were without premise, and it was apparent he had little knowledge of police investigations. The things he was saying was entirely community gossip and without any basis. However, I held my tongue and told him to continue. This was not how I would normally act, but I had practiced for a time such as this.

In truth, I had just finished reading a great book by Philip Yancey called, *What's So Amazing About Grace?*, and as this gentleman was spouting off, I was applying some of the techniques he had talked about in his book. How do you think this falls on the R-Y-G scale? I gave myself a Green. What about you?

Lincoln and Humility

Of all the people who could be mentioned here, I think Abraham Lincoln, the 16th president of the United States of America, would have to be one example of great humility.

Born in 1809 as the second son of Thomas and Nancy Hanks Lincoln, he was raised in a one-room log cabin on Sinking Spring Farm near Hodgenville, Kentucky. From these humble beginnings, Lincoln rose to be an example and model of virtue that stands out perhaps more than any other person in history.

Lincoln stands out for his outstanding accomplishments as a leader and perhaps more importantly—for the character qualities so famously attributed to him. But as great as he was, he was not born with those virtues—they had to be learned, honed, practiced, and developed daily, just as we should do.

Lincoln was far from a perfect individual. He possessed human flaws and made many mistakes in his life, as we all do. However, he learned from his mistakes and learned how to compensate for his shortcomings.

No matter who Abraham Lincoln met with, he believed to his core that all people deserve equal treatment. Through constant practice and diligent effort, even when Lincoln attained the president's great political position, he treated others he encountered with honesty, humility, courage, justice, and grace.

In one incident during President Lincoln's difficult presidency and the American Civil War, his secretary of war, Edwin McMasters Stanton, opposed an order that the president had issued. Another member of the government relates that when Stanton heard the order from the president, he was indignant. This order would exchange soldiers from the east and the west of the country to help them work effectively. Stanton asked for confirmation that Lincoln had given the order. When it was confirmed, Stanton said, "Then he is a fool."

When this statement was taken to Lincoln by the congressman whom Stanton had spoken to, the president said, "Did Stanton say I was a fool?" The congressman said, "He did, sir, and repeated it." Lincoln paused a moment, then replied, "If Stanton said I was a fool, then I must be one, for he is nearly always right and generally says what he means. I will step over and see him."

This is an excellent example of Lincoln's greatness—he was able to rise above his sensitivity and break away from others' opinions, even concerning himself. He accepted, even welcomed, criticism and demonstrated a strength in leadership that few leaders can achieve.

Lincoln is an excellent example of a humble man with excellent self-control. If you want to select a strong leader whose lead you should follow—he would be an excellent choice.

Chapter 15

THE KITCHEN SINK: A LITTLE BIT OF EVERYTHING IMPORTANT

We've covered quite a lot of ground in this book, and we've touched on quite a few different topics along the way. But there are many more things that we should talk about, and I'd like to take this chapter to clean up a few of these topics.

To be a healthy, wholesome person is a piece of the leadership puzzle. How you look physically, how you present yourself, and your appearance will all affect your staying power and energy. Some of these thoughts take great discipline every day.

To live a successful life, all these components must be present.

Dress for Success

Every day when you get up, it's an important step to think about how best to present yourself. How you appear to others is a large part of projecting leadership.

In this day of dressing down, most true professionals always look their best. If you are overweight and dress sloppily, this makes a statement to the people you are working with—and it's usually not a good one. You can be overweight, but dress professionally and make a far better statement.

We've all heard the phrase, "Don't judge a book by its cover," but the fact of the matter is that, no matter how wrong it might be to assess a person on first appearances, it still happens. First impressions are significant, and appearance is a big part of that first impression.

No matter what time or frame of life you are in, get up each day, shower, do your hair, shave (if applicable), and make sure you dress well and look professional. I'm not saying every day should require a shirt and tie, but try to look your best, even in casual attire.

How you dress, look, and feel makes a significant impact on your day. This is validated by a study that looked at students who went to school in a uniform every day and those who came in whatever clothing they thought best for the day. Guess which group excelled? I'm sure you can guess, but—the uniform group.

Wear great clothes. You never know whom you'll meet! Clothes make a strong, visual statement about how you see yourself.

During my law enforcement career, I would often mention this to the people who worked for me. "I would like you to tell me who you would like to talk to, the policeman who comes up beside your car who is overweight and sloppy with egg on his tie, or the policeman who is fit, polished, and professional?"

In your everyday life, I know you don't have to put a shirt and tie on, but always look your best, be dressed in neat, clean clothes, work at your appearance, have your hair trimmed and neat—overall, look like you mean business. Do this for your spouse and family, too. I get up every day and dress in clean clothes that fit and look the best for my spouse and family.

If you start with this one little nugget, you will notice a big difference.

What are the steps that you can take today to dress for success?

Exercise

You don't have to kill yourself at the gym to be healthy and physically fit. Walking is probably one of the best exercises you can do. It's good for your cardiovascular system and all your muscles, and it is relatively easy on your joints.

The big thing today seems to be going to the gym every day for an hour. While that's good for some, it may not be the easiest for you. Do your best to figure out another way to get exercise. Walk to work if you can or park some distance away from the office so you can stretch your legs getting there and back.

While you do this, though, remember that as we age, things do change. The things you wanted to do when you were 20 aren't necessarily the things you want to—or can do—when you hit 40, 50, or beyond.

We can all come up with excuses not to exercise. Do your best not to, though—try to get some exercise every day.

Blake is a motivational speaker from Sydney, Australia, and he tries to follow his routine every day. In one story he tells of one Sunday when he arrived home at 1 a.m. According to his practice, he gets up most days at 5 a.m. to head for the gym. This particular Sunday, the alarm went off, and he tried to talk himself into staying in bed—but ultimately, he got up to go for a run. He knew that a crack in his armor would result in him not meeting his goal and potentially could lead to him breaking out of his exercise program.

Exercise regularly—it's one great way to stay calm in stressful jobs. If it's difficult, find yourself a mentor to help with your program.

Most gyms have people on staff to mentor and help you through your program and progress if you choose to go. You can also find outstanding programs online to help, but many people want to do it independently. To those people, I recommend this: you need an accountability partner. If you don't find someone to hold you accountable, you are more likely to fail, and your results will be poor.

Staying focused on your goal is huge as well. Keep locked on that target. Remember, if you go outside and shoot arrows into the sky randomly, you're not going to hit anything; but if you keep a laser focus, you will hit the target—and eventually score that elusive bullseye!

Results are the ultimate acid test. If you are getting unsatisfactory results, you need a new plan, a new target. Targets are a big part of leadership success—I think you see that throughout this book, don't you?

Just keep in mind that results take time, and if you achieve immediate results, let this motivate you to keep moving forward. Project out into the future to see where you should be in a month, two months, six months, and so on. Write it down and keep it in mind. It's just another way to help train yourself to live every day with purpose—and when you live every day with purpose, you will succeed.

To sum up on this topic, getting exercise every day is important no matter how you do it. You can take advantage of the gym, walk, ride a bike, do push-ups at home, or whatever, but just make sure you keep moving. If necessary, with motivation, take advantage of the various programs and assistance available wherever you go—there are people at gyms who can help with that.

It all comes down to the energy you have—and don't you like being around energetic people? Remember the rule that the top five people you surround yourself with are the person you become—so be in the company of people who bring out the best in you.

I've been there myself. When someone can help you be the best you can be, it is incredible. Make a decision: decide to be above average. It's a big commitment, but it's far better than living your life on autopilot.

Raise your energy, look up lots, smile, and live your life on purpose. Remember: a healthy body means a healthy mind.

Your Diet: The 80/20 Rule

One rule that can help you stay healthy is the 80/20 rule. It's a way to approach your diet that ensures you're getting the most that you can out of your food while keeping some of the more troublesome parts of food away.

Our world today is full of processed food loaded with sugar, wheat, and other substances you can't name—or, if you can name them, you can't pronounce. You can thank advertising for that. Many of us grew up with the constant blare of breakfast cereal ads telling us that sugary blobs of wheat were good for us. We know better these days.

Do you know how many people think that fries are a vegetable? Food is an area of our lives that we should learn far more about, but a place where many people are less knowledgeable.

Preparing food at home from fresh ingredients and controlling your portion sizes can be very important for good health. By fresh foods, I mean very fresh—if you can manage it, buy all of your food locally. These foods will be the best in nutrition because they haven't had to travel long distances, haven't been frozen, and haven't been processed like many other foods might.

It is also important to talk about the difference between protein and carbohydrates and the amounts we need daily. Fats, as well, are an area that has been discussed incorrectly many times. Your body needs healthy fats as fuel to run well. The wrong kind of fat is one thing, but good fats are necessary for your everyday diet as they help with digestion and many other bodily functions.

Vitamins and nutrients are key to a healthy body and mind. So, do you dip your toe into purchasing supplements? They're a multibillion-dollar industry these days, but do we need them? Well, some are useful. Others are just good at making expensive urine. In some places and some cases, you may need a vitamin D supplement to ensure you're getting enough along with what's in your food, but I advocate for getting your vitamins from the source by eating fresh fruits and vegetables.

It's a good idea to eat cleanly—whole food, food that's still "alive" and hasn't had the nutrition processed out of it. It depends on your preferences how you approach this. Some people might go for a vegetarian diet, for example, and eat nothing but vegetables they get fresh; while others like myself prefer to have some meat in their diet. Work on finding the right mix for yourself and your lifestyle, and you'll help yourself out in the long run. Be careful, though. There are all kinds of fad diets out there that press different ideas and, for the most part, they are put out there by people trying to take advantage of you and make a buck.

Food doesn't need to be boring, either. There are so many good recipes and ideas out there today, foods from many different cultures that are tasty and healthy—hop on the Internet, look up something that you might like, and give it a shot.

A big part of this message is to ditch the junk food. Yes, it tastes great, and I love junk myself, but I know it's no good for me, and I try to keep myself healthy.

Hydration also helps, along with good food choices. Eating smarter and drinking enough fluids will make a big difference in your stress levels at work and home. How much hydration is a topic of some discussion; everyone has an opinion on it. Do some research on your own and see what the experts say on how much to drink for optimum health. (Or just use the pee test…if your urine is dark, you might be dehydrated, and if it's clear, you're probably okay!)

Try to stay away from fluids that are heavily sweetened or contain high amounts of sugar. Soda, heavily concentrated juices, and other similar drinks are a bad idea at the best of times. Instead, I stick to plain old water—maybe with a bit of essential oil included. Again, look at your options and do what you need to for your situation.

Here's a great idea. Keep a food and drink diary for a short period of time—say, a week or two—and then review what you ate during that stretch. I guarantee you'll be surprised to see just what you ate, and how much of it. This gives you a baseline for your health and lets you know what might need to be reevaluated. Read it and make the necessary changes to get those wonderful results we are looking for.

Fasting

We've established that good food and drink help reduce stress, and reducing stress is part of reaching our goals, which allows us as leaders to keep things going. Here's another thing we can consider in helping with our dietary efforts: fasting.

So many people overeat, and usually, they're overeating the wrong foods too. Overeating is a big problem for many people—I can't get into all of the issues that it can cause here because I'd need to write another book. (Many people have written those books already, honestly—research this yourself, it will prove interesting!)

I believe that fasting is an excellent tool in your dietary toolkit. It can offer many benefits, including weight control and overall vitality.

So, how does it work? Well, you can eat for eight hours a day and fast for 16 (intermittent fasting), or you could eat for five days and fast for two—it's really up to you. Information abounds on this topic, and you can pick up any number of books on the subject or search through websites, depending on your preference. I'm not sure that a long fast is a great idea because it doesn't seem natural to me for some reason; a body without fuel is like a car without gas—it doesn't work well and quits running. But the same can be said for too much fuel—the car becomes sluggish and spews black smoke, and the body decides to slow down your digestive tract, let the food ferment, and cause a multiplicity of problems. But eat just the right amount and both will run well. That analogy is so simple—it is that simple and not always so easy to do. It is something I continually work at.

Wisdom says this might be a topic to research closely. I like the 16/8 model, but that's what works for me—what works for you might be far different.

Remove Clutter from Your Life

Clutter is all around us. I learned this fact recently from my mentor: clutter lessens your productivity and keeps cycles open. (I'll explain cycles in a moment!) I never thought of that being the case, but it seems that this is accurate.

Many researchers have proven that physical clutter at home or the workplace negatively affects productivity. A cluttered desk or office can negatively affect your mood, resilience, and ability to work productively. Disorder and clutter create stress, which can cause low moods, low energy, and low vibration.

Even a very cluttered home can provoke emotional and mental distress, mainly because its occupants feel like they have no control over their spaces and, therefore, their lives.

Now: cycles. When we refer to open cycles, they often are defined as commitments made to yourself or to another person that haven't yet been fulfilled. These cycles hang out in your brain, using and draining your energy—lots of it. Think of what happens when you have many apps open on your phone at the same time and what that does to your battery life—well, that's what open cycles in your mind can do to you.

How do you break out of open cycles? Well, here are a few ideas to help.

- Identify what can be done in two minutes or less – What can you do in the next two minutes to reduce open cycles?
- Figure out what can be delegated – What can you delegate right away?
- Block out time for big decisions – Can you delegate time now for some big decisions today?
- Identify the best time to work on more significant projects – When is the best time to work on some other projects that you have?

Learn Words to Grow in Leadership

Here's an interesting thought for you. If you learned one new word every day, you could make a massive change in your life in one month and a dynamic change in your life in just one year.

Several concepts apply here. First, it is amazing how many people use words, and they don't know what the word means. A friend of mine, for example, loves the word chartreuse. He used this word in every sentence that he could. But here's the thing: he thought that chartreuse was another word for purple. He was amazed to see that chartreuse is actually a brilliant yellow green! He was taken aback, thinking of all the years he thought, incorrectly, about the word chartreuse—and other words as well. He changed his thinking, and now he looks up words often—and has made a contest of it with his daughter.

Learn one new word every day, and in five minutes or less a day, you will see results. It's quite impressive, really. The average person learns 25 new words or less each year, and their actual speaking vocabulary is about 400 words. One new word a day will give you a distinct advantage over most people you associate with or deal with in just one year. In five years, it will be a colossal advantage.

A more extensive vocabulary will give you a greater understanding of things that will enrich your life every day. There is also a bonus to this approach…every word you learn has a buddy, or buddies, that will expand your vocabulary even more. Fantastic idea, isn't it?

Zig Ziglar tells a story about expanding one's vocabulary, which illustrates this concept nicely.

A fellow named Vince Robert, from Ottawa, Ontario, was a fifth-grade dropout. At the age of 37, he was driving a taxi, and every day he spent many hours waiting for fares at hotels and airports—with plenty of downtime on his hands.

One day, he was taken by inspiration and bought himself a dictionary. He put it in his taxi on the seat next to him and started learning new words every day. As he did, his knowledge increased—and so did his confidence.

Eventually, that confidence boost led him to invest in the stock market, and soon he wound up buying his own taxi company.

Vince went on to lecture others on how to become successful.

Doesn't that make you want to grab the dictionary right away?

Profanity—Don't Bother

The use of profanity in everyday conversation has become commonplace, especially with Gen Xers and millennials, but others as well. The strange thing to me is that profanity doesn't add or bring any value to one's words; in fact, it almost exclusively detracts from the message.

We can all point to well-known politicians and celebrities that all too often use profanity in their daily dialogue. It seems to have become a badge of honor for many.

The use of profanity in the workplace also deserves to be mentioned. It seems today, when profanity is used in the workplace, managers and supervisors are reluctant to address it because it is feared that they will be seen as easily shocked or part of the speech police. However, leaders need to carefully consider their response to profane or obscene language used by employees and even themselves.

Virtually every workplace will have several employees who use crude, obscene, or profane language. This may sometimes include supervisors. Many workplaces will also have employees who find such language deeply offensive and abusive.

Balancing those competing concerns while at the same time staying in compliance with all relevant laws can be a tricky task. Employers must actively address the issue before significant problems arise.

Ignoring obscene or crude language can harm customer relations, cause the business to appear unprofessional, and even worse, put employers at risk of claims of allowing a hostile work environment.

To put it simply: bad language and profanity are a firm Red on the R-Y-G scale.

Motivational speaker Les Brown puts it well:

"Avoid foul-mouthed people. If you're one of them, commit to losing this part of yourself. Don't allow yourself to be a vessel or a sponge for filthy or disrespectful language or garbage disposal for violent words—especially from people supposed to love you. Some people enjoy using profanity, even when talking to children or when in their presence. Many people pay to listen to foul-mouthed rappers, comedians, and various entertainers. However, the acceptance of this as normal only speaks to our loss of spirituality and self-respect. It highlights the tragic lowering of our standards for language, which has negatively impacted our children.

"Cursing is the strongest expression of a weak mind. Don't fool yourself! Death and life are in the tongue. Your words create your world, and your world reflects your reality. You always have a choice. Use words that represent the highest and best expression of yourself, and of what you see for your future and your life."

Here is a great nugget of wisdom to file away—when in doubt, leave it out. If you have to ask other people whether something might be offensive to your audience, then that's probably a sign that there's the potential for it to be so.

This doesn't go for just profanity, either; use that rule for stories or comments that may also negatively affect someone.

Have a Sense of Humor

As I think back over my career, all the great leaders I ever worked for could make me laugh when things were going the wrong way. This doesn't mean they were jokesters or insensitive; they enjoyed a sense of honor and used it to enhance the workplace.

Leaders with honor can build stronger cultures, unleash more creativity, and even negotiate better deals. It seems like a sense of honor is an often-overlooked quality in leadership. It doesn't seem quite as important as communication, efficiency, and knowledge, but it is undoubtedly a prime piece of being a great leader. If you can inject a little more honor into your day, you, your employees, your family, your boss, and your coworkers will be happier and less stressed.

When things go south, as they sometimes will, try a chuckle. When things go wrong, instead of panicking, try to laugh. Sometimes the only thing to do during a disaster is to laugh and shrug at your luck.

Consider this: if you take five minutes to laugh, will it set your productivity back all that much? A great line to use is, "Isn't that interesting?" It could change a very tense, panicky moment in your association to something memorable.

Think about this point from a study I've just looked through. Employees who laugh at work tend to be healthier and more productive, but they are also absent from work less often. Further, honor has been shown to increase our ability to make decisions and make them quickly, think creatively, and solve complex problems—all of which can make for more productive, innovative, and profitable organizations.

Tips for Good Workplace Honor

It's not whether or not you're funny; it's what kind of funny you are. Be honest and authentic. If you can't be "ha-ha" funny, at least be "aha!" funny. Cleverness can be good enough.

Good comedy can be a secret plan, an inhouse secret created in your group. Don't be afraid to chuckle at yourself. It signals everything is okay. Laughter is disarming. Poke fun at the stuff everyone's worried about.

Spirituality, Faith, and Imagination

Proverbs 18:16 says, "When you exercise your gifts, the world makes room for you,[15] but it will also pay you for it." This is an interesting statement and particularly important for you as a leader. Consider that God has given you gifts to use for His glory. You may think to yourself, *I'm not important enough for God to give me a gift, skill, or talent.* Moving a step, we need to understand that our gifts are unique to each of us. Don't compare yourself by looking at what someone else can do and wish that were you. Remember the Harry Bicknell interview—comparison is deadly. Here is a question. How will your gift make room for you and bring you before great men? Here is the answer—the more you use your gift, the bigger it gets. It's like an exercised muscle that gets more robust and more powerful each time it is used. With practice, as you become excellent in your gift, others notice it, and as you prove trustworthy, doors will open for you that you could never imagine.

Alexander Graham Bell once believed that sound could be converted into electrical impulses and transmitted by wire.

No one remembers now, but many thought he was crazy. Now we remember only the man who had the vision and created the telephone. It is important to exercise your gifts and become a master at them.

In this book, we are working on your gift of leadership and how to master it. You can do it. If you do things half-measure, you can always find a job somewhere and do just enough to get by; you will remain simply an employee. If you decide that you will find something truly yours, you will fulfill your vision, and others will remember you.

Here are a few simple things you may want to consider to find your gift:

Do what you absolutely love to do.

Do what people ask more of from you. Is it because you are a great mechanic, a great cook? What is it that you do that makes people beg for more of your skill?

Think and figure out what that one thing is that you do better than everybody and that you love to do. I believe that chances are, this might be your unique gift to the world.

The Kitchen Sink of Leadership

By Robert Verbree

What do we mean by the kitchen sink?
In the leadership world, is it that which you drink?
Well, maybe in a sense it is.
Let's continue on with this interesting quiz.
This starts each day with your decision, your mindset, and philosophy.
Do you wake up from sleep alive or to a cacophony?
Of alarms or cell phones, radio or TV,
Is it gallons of coffee, an energy drink, maybe?
Come on now, which is true?
Are you changing it up, or just part of the group
Who run on the hamster wheel of the tyranny of the urgent,
Never smelling the flowers and constant stress that's recurrent?
As your day gets underway, consider your energy number.
Do you think of the gym, or a walk; is it more slumber?
Best be off for my workout; do you think out loud,
That stress to release, to be ahead of the crowd?
Next, how will I look when I enter the pen?
Will I be showered and ready for when
I meet my first contact,
Be it, Husband or Wife, the kids or the mailman?
We meet so many in life.
Always look your best, be it in casual or professionally dressed.
First impressions say lots; let the first one be best.
You are what you eat has been said by many.
Let food be your medicine,

The ultimate remedy.

Do you overeat? Is it wholesome food, or fast-food junk?

'Cause the engine needs fuel

Not a big processed lump,

Which causes all sorts of internal distress,

From aching knees to depression and unable to jest.

Better to eat less, and fast if you please.

Your body will thank you, especially your knees.

What about clutter from life's daily progression?

The things that don't matter,

You must learn to jettison.

From the noise that social media brings

To the cluttered drawers and open cycles which sing.

Take time for a breather and position yourself

In a place that is peaceful, which centering brings.

Profanity and bad language overflow from the heart,

People who partake are really not smart.

It detracts from your message

And brings zero value.

Best learn some new words

And grow up from what's shallow.

It is proven that the more words you know, the greater your worth.

You'll be more employable with an enviable berth.

Your honor says so much about you,

Your ability to laugh at yourself or your crew.

Leaders who know this tend to keep all things light.

And when the storm hits, everyone is all right.

Another gift which all great leaders bring

Is spirituality, faith, and imagining.

These qualities bring wisdom, vision, and insight,
And help you understand the things that are right.
Now, let's close this poem with a perilous thought.
Great leadership takes work;
Great leaders are sought.
So where will you land, mediocre or best?
Will the work you have done be up to the test?
Have you been a coward in the leadership fight?
Have you turned right from wrong?
Consider well how you might move it along.

Chapter 16

STATESMAN, MAN OF COURAGE, PATIENCE, AND DISCIPLINE

Nehemiah

'd like to share one more interview with you before we wrap up this book. It's a bit different from the previous leaders I have introduced you to. The subject is a little older, for one, and he lived a very long time ago. He is an excellent example of how leadership has remained quite similar from one millennium to the next.

Nehemiah[16] was a Jewish man, born during the time of the Babylonian exile from Judah. He lived in the fifth century BC and served under the Persian King Artaxerxes I.

Not a lot is known about his early years, but we must rightfully assume that he was intelligent, sharp, efficient, wise, and focused to a fault. Under Nehemiah's leadership, the Jews withstood opposition and came together to accomplish their goal.

Nehemiah led by example, giving up a respected position in a palace for hard labor in a politically insignificant district. He was the cupbearer for the king; he was essentially a bodyguard who spent much of his time with the king and probably spent mealtimes with Artaxerxes at the very least.

Today, Nehemiah would be called a veteran statesman.

One of his major responsibilities was to taste the king's wine to make sure it wasn't poisoned. In scripture, we are also told he was the king's trusted friend and advisor, and they knew each other personally. The king would know when Nehemiah was troubled.

Around 446 or 445 BC, his brother, Hanani, came to visit from Judea. He brought disturbing news about the terrible conditions the Jewish people were facing after being allowed to return home from exile to Jerusalem some years earlier. This was incredibly distressing to Nehemiah, and he prayed for a long time for an opportunity to be able to speak to the king.

He remained patient over four months before the opportunity came. The king noticed that he was downcast in his presence, which we can suspect must have been strange for Nehemiah, and the king asked him what was wrong. He explained, and the king listened.

After his conversations with Artaxerxes, Nehemiah was appointed to be Judea's governor and sent there with an escort. His mission was to rebuild the walls around the city and restore some order there. After arriving there, he immediately rallied the people and began organizing work teams for the task.

Nehemiah was a man who would not begin until he counted the cost and would not stop until a task was completed. Every trade, business, or large family was assigned a portion of the city wall to repair.

But before long, opposition rose to the surface. Certain nobles refused to stoop to manual labor on the walls. Leaders of the people surrounding Jerusalem threatened Nehemiah and his workers and attacked them while they worked. Nehemiah had to arm half the workers and assign them guard duty while the other half labored.

He faced powerful opposition from Sanballat and Tobiah, who tried their utmost to impede the rebuilding of the walls.

What is very notable here is this: Nehemiah was not deterred from his goal. He had a firm resolve. His enemies scoffed at his attempts to get the job done, threatened to attack the workmen, and even threatened to take his life—and yet, amazingly, Nehemiah got the wall completed in 52 days.

In rebuilding Jerusalem, Nehemiah faced many key problems: ridicule, wrath, discouragement, fear, internal strife, laziness, compromise, and lying. He was not alone in these challenges. Most, if not all, people in leadership will experience these in some form or another.

The truth is that few men exemplify the strength of character, faith, and trust in God that he exhibited. Nehemiah was an excellent leader and a model for today.

In keeping with the other interview stories in this book, I want to ask the same questions I asked each person I interviewed, as if Nehemiah were present, and record his "thoughts" on leadership.

Nehemiah positions his leadership as being pacesetting, democratic, coaching, and affirmative. He is most certainly not laissez-faire, autocratic, or command-and-control. Working with Judah's people, he likes the collaborative leadership style, which is inclusive and brings value to all involved. His motives and goals are God-centered and God-driven.

Now, let's look at how Nehemiah would feel about some of our other key points explored in this book.

In terms of self-talk, Nehemiah always talked to himself in the positive and was upbeat before the king. He was deeply devoted to God and what God wanted. He was very concerned for the king's affairs, whom he worked for, and called to a life of good works. At the same time, he showed great concern for his nation and its people's well being.

Nehemiah's mindset, I feel, was that there were many people far more qualified than he was. I believe he honestly felt that way. He was only asked to do his best and let God take care of the details, and that was his mindset. He worked at not getting caught up in the comparison trap and likely knew that comparison was deadly.

For a life philosophy, Nehemiah seems to have been content to be a servant, be a blessing, and encourage everyone to be their best. His mission was to lead the people from Judah and encourage them to rebuild the wall, which had been demolished. He had a firm resolve to get this completed and a complete faith that God would be helping him, at his side.

Testing and talking to people to learn where they are coming from and understanding them is very important. Know and listen, so you don't initially write them off. I'm sure that Nehemiah was able to manage this and understand the struggles of his people.

People who want to wage war upon you are indeed classified as "difficult" in my book, and Nehemiah handled them well. He used extra grace to love the people who irritated him. You should not give in to their threats and intimidation. Have a strong resolve to complete the task you have in your mind. Do not be afraid to stand up against those who oppose you and what you want to accomplish.

Nehemiah—Interview Insights

- Patience is a virtue.
- Spirituality is an excellent quality for a leader.
- One must have a steadfast resolve and strong determination.
- A good leader works with his people.
- A good leader stands up for his people.
- A good leader brings out the best in his people.
- A life of discipline is a must for a great leader. (15)

Chapter 17

AWARENESS

Well, you made it! Here it is—the end of the book.

We started this journey with a truckload of stress at the office, and maybe at home, with friends, or family. Now, with what you've learned in these pages, you should have a good start at honing the skills that will dial all of that stress back substantially.

Let's face it, though—the chances of all those high-pressure issues totally leaving are small, and it probably won't happen. But you're now better equipped to handle them when they do arise.

So, where have we been on this journey? Well, let's see. We talked about making a plan. How about changing your mindset? Yes, that was in there as well—and so was being the change.

I remember reading about a woman who worked at a low-paying job all her life, but at retirement, she was a multimillionaire, able to live on a cruise ship for her retirement years and see the entire world. That speaks volumes about her mindset, as well as her focus to make the changes necessary. It didn't happen overnight—but happen it did. That speaks to changing things up, having a plan, and to be ready to face the challenges that leadership brings.

In telling these stories and sharing these tips and tricks, I wanted to take you from one side of the river to the other, using these concepts as steppingstones.

Now, let's have a little pep talk before we sign off.

My intention for this book was to give you a little manual that you can use every day. I have noticed that so many books on management are thick and laborious. That's not to say they aren't valuable, but there are times when we need a quick start that can set us on the road to making a difference. My hope is what I have done for you here can give you just that—the directions to put your feet on the right path.

So where are you going from here? What are you going to do with this information? Many people will lay this book down, and that will be the end of it.

I'd like to see you commit right now. If you have decided to change, do it right away, and start by turning to the last page of this book. There's space there for you to write these words: I will make a change, and I am going to start right away.

Go ahead—I'll wait for you to get back. This is too important for me not to!

Ah, you're back! How do you feel? Is your energy up? Will you be the change? Are you going to make a difference, despite the critics who will come your way?

Go out and live your life now with focus and drive, and may your stress be near zero on the dial. I know you can do it.

Recognizing Those Positive Circumstances— Opportunity

Recognizing opportunities to build and better the team is an excellent piece of the management puzzle. Attempts to analyze all the what, where, why, when, who, and how leadership works are often misplaced. These studies often examine showmanship or power, how to move up the corporate ladder, wisdom or popularity, and maybe planning.

My studies lead me to believe that this statement is correct. Leadership does not just center on achievers and achievement. It is so much more.

Top-down management is a failed leadership style. It may have to be used in a crisis over the short term, but it must not be your management style's overarching component. We want to become better leaders. Becoming a better leader, using shared responsibility, and promoting teamwork will move your mission forward.

When you lead with a worldview that the janitor is just as important as the assistant manager, you will see enviable results. This is your time to improve every day.

Leaving a Legacy

Act despite your fear. Most of us have great ideas, but within seconds of thinking about it, we talk ourselves out of it because of "the can'ts." Instead, act and be the change.

Earlier in this book I said if you don't act within four seconds of your epiphany, you will talk yourself out of it. I think this is something we've all experienced at least once in our lives. Being the change because you have had a great idea is very important. So many people go to their graves with their music still in them.

Les Brown has often said that many people die when they are 25
and go to their graves when they are 65. I do believe there is an element
of truth to this. So, don't strive to be average—strive to be the best you
can be, and live your life to the fullest. This will take energy, but having
energy is so good. Don't you prefer to be around energetic people, as
opposed to those who are humdrum and laissez-faire? I certainly am—
please, release me from those who can't get it started!

I was at a seminar recently, and an elderly lady, who was perhaps in
her late 70s or early 80s, was there. She was electric. When I came into
the room, she was talking to younger people about rock music, and the
next thing I knew, she had her phone out and was dancing to "Gloria"
by the Doors. Wow, wow, and wow—what energy! I loved it, and so did
everybody else in the room. Positive energy is absolutely infectious.

Who Cares

Don't worry—I'm going to let go of your hand very soon.

This book is all about some things you can put in place to turn
down the stress volume at work, at home, and anywhere you lead. You'll
have to fly on your own soon. First, though, we need to talk about "who
cares." This affects many of us. Of course, some people just don't care.
They are all about themselves and not at all interested in relationships
and the greater good.

You, though—you know there is an audience out there for what
you're sharing. In this case, it's your leadership that they want. There are
people out there who care, and when you develop an atmosphere of trust
and cohesiveness at your workplace, it will become infectious.

There are always critics—remember our analogy earlier of fruit
producers and fruit pickers. The critics are usually in the latter group,
aren't they?

This seems to be a universal truth: no matter what the topic, someone will not see it the way you do. Sometimes you can win them over, but there are times when you just cannot. Trying to beat those critics smoothly goes into detail that is far more than I can cover in this book—but maybe it can wait for another day. Know, though, that you will be criticized if you want to step out and be a leader, especially one who is all about change.

I encourage you with this: don't lose your stride. Some critics will want to knock you off your horse because they see you are more successful than they are. Often they're just jealous and want to see you fail. Don't react to these people; just respond. The difference between the two is simple: reacting is negative and responding is positive.

Be Aware

Awareness undergirds excellence. To excel in leadership, a person must be aware of all the elements that contribute to excellent performance and continuously measure their performance against the standard they have set for themselves.

Leadership is the discipline of deliberately exerting special influence within a group to move it towards beneficial permanence that fulfills the group's needs. Remember this definition; it's a perfect one to keep in mind.

Five Points to Keep in Mind About Leadership:

- Leadership is a discipline; it takes hard work, effort, concentration, and staying power.
- Leadership is deliberate; a great leader leaves nothing to chance.
- Leadership exerts a special influence that is geared to change and improve lifestyle.

- Leadership sets the goals of beneficial permanence.
- Leadership focuses on fulfilling real needs.

Let's quickly review the chapters in this book to emphasize and be aware of the importance of each piece.

You must decide quickly to act. Many have great ideas but talk themselves out of it in four seconds or less.

Your self-talk is the way you talk to yourself every second of every day. You start to learn your self-talk early in life, affecting how you live your entire life.

Your mindset, your thoughts, beliefs, and expectations are the lenses through which you perceive the world. Your mindset can be either fixed or growth—which brings challenges or opens and accepts new information and learning.

Your life philosophy is the major determining factor in how your life works out. Your life philosophy is a mental framework for understanding how the world works and how you fit into the world.

Relationships form a huge part of the leadership puzzle; they can make or break it.

Mentoring is essential to moving forward and succeeding in your leadership. All great leaders have a mentor.

One Last Time: Great Leaders

- Great leaders invest in their team.
- Great leaders say, "Let's go do it"; they have a clear vision, a defined mission, and are great at goal setting.
- Great leaders know and listen to their people.
- Great leaders learn about their people by testing them so they can work on their gifts.

- Great leaders trust their people and delegate responsibility freely to help everyone feel like they are an important and integral part of the team.
- Great leaders can handle difficult people and don't take criticism personally.
- Great leaders are very disciplined.
- Great leaders study how it is done and have mastered great communication.
- Great leaders have high integrity.
- Great leaders are wise and look to build wisdom.
- Great leaders have great self-control.
- Great leaders have true humility—humility gives tensile strength to leadership.
- Great leaders dress for success.
- Great leaders exercise.
- Great leaders eat a balanced diet.
- Great leaders remove clutter from their lives.
- Great leaders grow in vocabulary every day.
- Great leaders avoid bad language and profanity at all costs.
- Great leaders have a sense of honor.
- Great leaders understand that your gift will make room for you.

EPILOGUE

This book started with a story so let's finish with a story. I do like great stories! From Matthew 13¹⁷ in the Bible, the parable of the sower is one of my favorites. Some call it the law of sowing and reaping.

As you read this story, you learn about an ambitious farmer who goes out to sow his seed. This ambitious farmer could be you, a great leader going out to lead the team and make a positive difference in your organization or your family. You begin to sow the seeds of leadership, and like the farmer in the story, some of the seed falls on the path or hard ground. The birds come and eat this seed—kind of like people who don't listen. Why don't people listen, you ask? These people should listen to good leadership advice. Well, it is just the way it is. It is part of the plan and part of the structure, and you can't change it. Some things you just can't change. The sun will come up tomorrow in the east, and it will set in the west; you can't control it. It is the same with those who will not listen; you can't control it. When there are people in your group like this, you must discipline yourself and not get upset, and not chase after them. A great statement to make when this happens would be, "Isn't that interesting?" So, know this; the birds are going to get some of the seed you sow.

As the story continues, the farmer keeps on sowing his seed, and some falls on rocky places where it doesn't have much soil. It sprang up quickly because the soil was shallow and warm, but when the noon sun came up, the plants were scorched by the heat, and they withered because they had no root. On the stony ground where there is little soil, the plants grow, but only for a short time—like people who hear what you have to say but don't listen to understand, probably because they aren't interested in real, lasting change. This will be hard to bear, but you must discipline yourself by saying something like, "Isn't that interesting?"—it's just the way it is. This is not of your doing or making. Some hear the message but aren't interested in really listening and applying it. It's just the way it is.

The farmer keeps on sowing his seed. Remember, the farmer has good seed, and he is ambitious. As he continues to sow the seed, some falls among the thorns. On the thorny ground, the plants grow but are later choked out by the weeds—kind of like people who hear your message but don't believe you and are consumed by others' opinions or critique. Thinking they know better, they forget the message you bring. These people are easily convinced to change their minds and often go with popular opinion. This will be hard to bear, but you must discipline yourself by saying something like, "Isn't that interesting?"—it's just the way it is. This is not of your doing or making. Some will hear what you have to say, but they will go off and do their own thing because they think they know much better how it is done on their own. Like the sun coming up in the east and setting in the west, it is totally out of your control. Respond by saying, "Isn't that interesting?" and understand some think they know much more than you do; it's just the way it is. It is part of the plan and part of the structure totally out of your control.

Our ambitious farmer keeps on sowing the seed. Some of the seed falls on good ground, producing a crop 100, 60, or 30 times what was sown. It is a fact if you keep on sowing the seed, it will always fall on good ground. If you share a good idea long enough or work on bettering your skills long enough, it will fall on the right people. The seed produces a bountiful crop on the fertile ground—like believing in the vision and being committed to that vision.

The message is simple. Start with ambition and excellent seed—your story. Keep on sowing the seed (persevere). Determination, patience, and the law of averages will carry you past the birds, the scorching sun, the thorns—to harvesttime!

Here is my closing thought—you can do the most remarkable things no matter what happens!

CALL TO ACTION
Go Forward and Lead

This is it. Go forward now and begin your journey. Remember: it won't happen in one day because change takes time. A difference of one degree today is a lot in one month, significant in a year, and huge in five years. The first step is to take action. Action trumps every other thing as long as it is the right action.

I truly hope this book has been the inspiration to get you started.

"I will make a change, and I am going to start right away."

Signed: _____

ABOUT THE AUTHOR

Robert J Verbree is a retired police officer. He was a peace officer in Canada's Royal Canadian Mounted Police (RCMP) for 35 years and retired in 2014. Robert is an award-winning author of the self-published and self-marketed book, *My Life as a Cop*. He has written a few chapters in the *Magnetic Entrepreneur* book series. He is currently working on another book with the working title *PTSD Survivors* which includes first-hand interviews of 30 PTSD survivors and how they have been able to push through and live a normal life again. Robert is an international speaker and currently has a consulting business helping to promote great leadership in the trucking industry.

He is married to Ruth Verbree and together they have three grown children and four grandchildren. He lives in Kamloops, British Columbia, Canada.

ADDITIONAL RESOURCES

Some Excellent Books on Leadership and Self-Development

1. *Man's Search for Meaning* by Viktor Frankl
   Originally Published in 1946
   ISBN-10: 9780807014271
   ISBN-13: 978-0807014271
   Publisher: Beacon Press; 1st edition (June 1, 2006)
2. *Think and Grow Rich* by Napoleon Hill
   Originally published in March 1937
   ISBN-10: 1546962514
   ISBN-13: 978-1546962519
   Publisher: CreateSpace Independent Publishing Platform; 1st edition (May 27, 2017)
3. *The 7 Habits of Highly Effective People* by Stephen R. Covey
   Originally published: 1989
   ISBN-10: 9781451639612
   ISBN-13: 978-1451639612

Publisher: Simon & Schuster; Anniversary edition (November 19, 2013)

4. *How to Win Friends & Influence People* by Dale Carnegie
    Originally published: October 1936
    ISBN-10: 0671027034
    ISBN-13: 978-0671027032
    Publisher: Gallery Books; Revised ed. edition (October 1, 1998)

5. *Leaders Eat Last* by Simon Sinek
    Originally published: 2014
    ISBN-10: 1591845327
    ISBN-13: 978-1591845324
    Publisher: Portfolio; Illustrated edition (January 7, 2014)

6. *he 21 Irrefutable Laws of Leadership* by John C. Maxwell
    Originally published: September 16, 1998
    ISBN-10: 0785288376
    ISBN-13: 978-0785288374
    Publisher: HarperCollins Leadership; 10th Anniversary Edition (September 16, 2007)

7. *The Power of Your Subconscious* Mind by Joseph Murphy
    Originally published: 1963
    ISBN-10: 0735204551
    ISBN-13: 978-0735204553
    Publisher: Prentice Hall Press; Revised edition (January 4, 2011)

8. *Principle-Centered Leadership* by Stephen R. Covey
    Originally published: April 1989
    ISBN-13: 978-1455893485
    ISBN-10: 145589348X
    Publisher: Franklin Covey on Brilliance Audio; Unabridged edition (April 1, 2012)

9. *Never Split the Difference* by Christopher Voss and Tahl Raz
    Originally published: May 17, 2016
    ISBN-10: 0062407805
    ISBN-13: 978-0062407801
    Publisher: Harper Business; 1st edition (May 17, 2016)
10. *Meditations* by Marcus Aurelius
    ISBN-10: 9780812968255
    ISBN-13: 978-0812968255
    Publisher: Modern Library; First American PB Edition (May 6, 2003)

This is a small list of great books to read on leadership and personal development.

I do encourage you to read widely and often.

ENDNOTES

1   *Leaders Eat Last: Why Some Teams Pull Together and Others Don't* by Simon Sinek, ISBN-13: 978-1591848011. Publisher: Portfolio; Illustrated edition (May 23, 2017)

2   Joshua 24:15, New International Version Bible

3   *Think and Grow Rich* (The Edwin C Barnes Story) by Napoleon Hill. Originally published in March 1937 https://www.bridgetostrength.com/articles/rags-to-riches—By Robert Drucker

4   *Man's Search for Meaning* by Viktor Frankl. Originally Published in 1946.

5   Proverbs, New International Version Bible

6   Proverbs 23:7, New International Version Bible

7   *Mover of Men and Mountains* by Robert Gilmour LeTourneau, ISBN-13: 978-0802438188. Publisher: Moody Publishers (June 1, 1967), https://en.wikipedia.org/wiki/R._G._LeTourneau

8   Thessalonians 5:16-18, New International Version Bible

9   *Biscuits, Fleas, and Pump Handles*, ISBN-13: 978-1598597059. Publisher: Oasis Audio; Unabridged edition (November 19, 2009)

10 James 13:3, New International Version Bible

11 Proverbs 9:10-12, New International Version Bible

12 Proverbs 9:10-12, New International Version Bible

13 https://en.wikipedia.org/wiki/The Jackie Robinson Story

14 https://drbiggie.wordpress.com/2018/03/04/billy-graham-chuck-templeton-and-bron-clifford

15 Proverbs 18:16, New International Version Bible

16 Nehemiah chapters 1 and 2, New International Version Bible

17 Matthew 13, New International Version Bible

A free ebook edition is available with the purchase of this book.

To claim your free ebook edition:

1. Visit MorganJamesBOGO.com
2. Sign your name CLEARLY in the space
3. Complete the form and submit a photo of the entire copyright page
4. You or your friend can download the ebook to your preferred device

Print & Digital Together Forever.

Snap a photo   Free ebook   Read anywhere